ARM Assembly Language Programming
Learn Through 100+ Examples

By Yury Magda

To my wife, Julia

About the Author

Yury Magda is an embedded engineer experienced in designing hardware and software for Intel x86, ARM and RISC-V embedded systems. He is also the author of the books on designing embedded systems based upon various development platforms.

Contents

Introduction

This book is designed as a hands-on guide for anyone interested in mastering ARM Assembly Language, one of the most widely used instruction sets in modern embedded systems and mobile devices.

Whether you're a student, an aspiring embedded system engineer, or a hobbyist eager to explore the low-level workings of ARM processors, this book will provide you with the foundational knowledge and practical skills you need. ARM Assembly Language can seem daunting at first, but with the right approach and plenty of examples to practice with, it becomes a powerful tool in your programming arsenal.

Why ARM Assembly?

ARM processors are ubiquitous in today's technology landscape. From smartphones and tablets to IoT devices and advanced microcontrollers, ARM's architecture powers a wide range of applications. Learning to program in ARM Assembly Language opens the door to optimizing software for performance and understanding the underlying hardware at a much deeper level.

What You'll Learn

This book takes a unique approach by focusing on learning through examples. With more than 100 carefully selected examples, each accompanied by detailed explanations, you'll gradually build up your understanding of ARM Assembly Language. The examples range from simple arithmetic operations to more complex algorithms, giving you a well-rounded introduction to the language.

Who This Book Is For

This book is intended for beginners who are new to assembly language programming. No prior experience with ARM Assembly is required. However, a basic understanding of programming concepts and familiarity with another programming language will be helpful as you work through the examples.

How to Use This Book

Each chapter introduces new concepts and techniques, followed by a set of examples that demonstrate their application. You are encouraged to work through these examples on your own, experimenting with the code and observing how it interacts with the ARM architecture. This hands-on approach will reinforce your learning and build your confidence as an ARM Assembly Language programmer.

Disclaimer

While the author has used good faith efforts to ensure that the information and instructions contained in this book are accurate, the author disclaims all responsibility for errors or omissions, including without limitation responsibility for damages resulting from the use of or reliance on this work. Use of the information and instructions contained in this work is at your own risk. If any code samples or other technology this book contains or describes is subject to open source licenses or the intellectual property rights of others, it is your responsibility to ensure that your use thereof complies with such licenses and/or rights. All example applications from this book were developed and tested without damaging hardware. The author will not accept any responsibility for damages of any kind due to actions taken by you after reading this book.

Basic concepts

The ARM Assembly Language is known for several key features that make it distinct and powerful, particularly in embedded systems and mobile computing. Here are the main features:

1. **RISC Architecture**
   - Reduced Instruction Set Computing (RISC): ARM processors use a RISC architecture, which means they have a small, highly optimized set of instructions. This leads to efficient execution and low power consumption, making ARM ideal for embedded and mobile applications.

2. **Uniform Instruction Length**
   - Fixed-Length Instructions: Most ARM instructions are 32 bits in length, which simplifies instruction decoding and allows for faster execution. The ARM Thumb instruction set, a subset of the full ARM instruction set, uses 16-bit instructions to improve code density.

3. **Load/Store Architecture**
   - Separate Data and Instructions: ARM Assembly uses a load/store architecture, meaning data must be loaded into registers before it can be processed. This keeps the instruction set simple and helps optimize performance.

4. **Large Register Set**
   - 16 General-Purpose Registers: ARM processors have 16 general-purpose registers (**R0** to **R15**), which can be used for a variety of purposes, such as holding operands for operations, storing temporary data, or holding addresses for memory access.

5. **Conditional Execution**
   - Conditional Instructions: Many ARM instructions can be conditionally executed based on the status flags in the Current Program Status Register (**CPSR**). This reduces the need for branching, leading to more efficient code.

6. **Flexible Addressing Modes**

- Multiple Addressing Modes: ARM provides a variety of addressing modes, such as immediate, register, and scaled register addressing. This flexibility allows for efficient memory access and manipulation.

7. Efficient Branching

- Branch and Link Instructions: ARM includes efficient branching instructions, such as `B` (branch) and `BL` (branch with link), which allow for function calls and returning from functions. The `BL` instruction also stores the return address in the link register (**LR**).

8. Support for Thumb and Thumb-2 Instruction Sets

- Compact Code: ARM processors support the Thumb and Thumb-2 instruction sets, which provide more compact 16-bit instructions, improving code density and efficiency, particularly in memory-constrained environments.

9. Pipeline Architecture

- Pipelined Execution: ARM processors typically use a pipeline architecture, allowing multiple instructions to be processed simultaneously at different stages of execution. This enhances performance by increasing instruction throughput.

10. Support for Co-Processors

- Extended Functionality: ARM architecture allows for the integration of co-processors, which can extend the instruction set and provide additional features, such as floating-point operations or advanced SIMD (Single Instruction, Multiple Data) processing.

11. Low Power Consumption

- Energy Efficiency: ARM's design focuses on minimizing power consumption, making it ideal for battery-powered devices and systems where energy efficiency is crucial.

12. Interrupt Handling

- Fast Interrupts: ARM processors provide efficient interrupt handling mechanisms, including fast interrupt requests (FIQ) and standard interrupt requests (IRQ), allowing for quick response to external events.

13. Software Interrupts (SWI)

- System Calls: ARM supports software interrupts, allowing user-mode programs to request services from the operating system or to perform system calls efficiently.

14. Floating-Point and NEON Support

- Advanced Processing: Many ARM processors include support for floating-point operations and NEON technology, which is an advanced SIMD architecture for accelerating multimedia and signal processing tasks.

15. Scalability

- Broad Use Cases: ARM Assembly Language is used across a wide range of devices, from low-power microcontrollers to high-performance processors in smartphones, tablets, and servers. This scalability makes ARM a versatile choice for various applications.

These features collectively contribute to ARM's dominance in the embedded systems and mobile device markets, making it an essential language to learn for those interested in low-level programming and system design.

ARM Instructions: a quick overview

ARM Assembly Language provides a variety of instructions that can be used for arithmetic operations, logical operations, data movement, comparison, and branching. Below is a quick overview of the main ARM instructions:

1. **Arithmetic Instructions**
   - **ADD** (Add): Adds two values and stores the result in a register.
     - ADD R0, R1, R2 ; R0 = R1 + R2
     - ADC (Add with Carry): Adds two values along with the carry flag and stores the result in a register.
     - ADC R0, R1, R2 ; R0 = R1 + R2 + Carry
   - **SUB** (Subtract): Subtracts one value from another and stores the result in a register.
     - SUB R0, R1, R2 ; R0 = R1 - R2
     - SBC (Subtract with Carry): Subtracts one value and the carry flag from another and stores the result in a register.
     - SBC R0, R1, R2 ; R0 = R1 - R2 - Carry
     - RSB (Reverse Subtract): Subtracts the first operand from the second operand and stores the result in a register.
     - RSB R0, R1, R2; R0 = R2 - R1
   - **MUL** (Multiply): Multiplies two values and stores the lower 32 bits of the result in a register.
     - MUL R0, R1, R2 ; R0 = R1 * R2
     - MLA (Multiply Accumulate): Multiplies two values, adds a third value, and stores the lower 32 bits of the result in a register.
     - MLA R0, R1, R2, R3 ; R0 = (R1 * R2) + R3

2. **Logical Instructions**
   - **AND** (Bitwise AND): Performs a bitwise AND operation between two values and stores the result in a register.
     - AND R0, R1, R2 ; R0 = R1 & R2
   - **ORR** (Bitwise OR): Performs a bitwise OR operation between two values and stores the result in a register.
     - ORR R0, R1, R2 ; R0 = R1 | R2
   - **EOR** (Bitwise Exclusive OR): Performs a bitwise exclusive OR (XOR) operation between two values and stores the result in a register.

- EOR R0, R1, R2 ; R0 = R1 ^ R2
- **BIC** (Bitwise Clear): Performs a bitwise AND operation between a value and the complement of another value, storing the result in a register.
  - BIC R0, R1, R2 ; R0 = R1 & ~R2
- **MVN** (Move NOT): Moves the bitwise complement of a value into a register.
  - MVN R0, R1 ; R0 = ~R1

3. Shift and Rotate Instructions

- **LSL** (Logical Shift Left): Shifts a value to the left by a specified number of bits, filling the vacated bits with zeros.
  - LSL R0, R1, #2 ; R0 = R1 << 2
- **LSR** (Logical Shift Right): Shifts a value to the right by a specified number of bits, filling the vacated bits with zeros.
  - LSR R0, R1, #2 ; R0 = R1 >> 2
- **ASR** (Arithmetic Shift Right): Shifts a value to the right by a specified number of bits, preserving the sign bit.
  - ASR R0, R1, #2 ; R0 = R1 >> 2 with sign extension
- **ROR** (Rotate Right): Rotates a value to the right by a specified number of bits.
  - ROR R0, R1, #2 ; R0 = R1 rotated right by 2 bits
- **RRX** (Rotate Right with Extend): Rotates a value to the right by one bit and extends the carry flag into the most significant bit.
  - RRX R0, R1 ; R0 = R1 rotated right by 1 bit with carry extension

4. Comparison Instructions

- **CMP** (Compare): Compares two values by subtracting the second value from the first, setting the condition flags based on the result.
  - CMP R1, R2 ; Compare R1 and R2 (sets flags)
- **CMN** (Compare Negated): Compares two values by adding the first value and the negation of the second, setting the condition flags based on the result.
  - CMN R1, R2 ; Compare R1 and -R2 (sets flags)
- **TST** (Test): Performs a bitwise AND operation between two values, setting the condition flags based on the result.
  - TST R1, R2 ; Test R1 & R2 (sets flags)

- **TEQ** (Test Equivalence): Performs a bitwise XOR operation between two values, setting the condition flags based on the result.
  - TEQ R1, R2 ; Test R1 ^ R2 (sets flags)

5. **Data Movement Instructions**
- **MOV** (Move): Copies a value into a register.
  - MOV R0, R1 ; R0 = R1
- **MVN** (Move NOT): Copies the bitwise complement of a value into a register.
  - MVN R0, R1 ; R0 = ~R1
- **LDR** (Load Register): Loads a value from memory into a register.
  - LDR R0, [R1] ; Load value at address R1 into R0
- **STR** (Store Register): Stores a value from a register into memory.
  - STR R0, [R1] ; Store R0 into memory at address R1

6. **Branching Instructions**
- **B** (Branch): Unconditionally branches to a specified label or address.
  - B target_label ; Branch to target_label
- **BL** (Branch with Link): Branches to a subroutine and saves the return address in the link register (LR).
- **BL subroutine_label** ; Branch to subroutine_label and save return address.
- **BX** (Branch and Exchange): Branches to an address and optionally switches between ARM and Thumb instruction sets.
  - BX R0 ; Branch to address in R0

Interfacing ARM assembly procedures with C code

To view the results of operations provided by assembly code, we will interface standalone assembly procedures with C code. Interfacing a standalone ARM assembly procedure with C code involves several steps, including writing the assembly procedure, declaring it in your C code, and ensuring that the calling conventions are correctly followed. Here's a step-by-step guide:

1. Write the ARM Assembly Procedure

Write your ARM assembly procedure in a separate file with a `.s` or `.asm` extension. Ensure that the procedure adheres to the ARM procedure call standard (AAPCS) or ARM EABI (Embedded Application Binary Interface), which dictates how functions should be called, how arguments are passed, and how the return values are handled.
Below (**Listing 1**) is an example of the assembly procedure (file **add_two_numbers.s**).

Listing 1.

```
.global add_two_numbers
add_two_numbers:
    ADD R0, R0, R1  // R0 = R0 + R1
    BX  LR          // Return to caller
```

This simple procedure adds two integers passed in registers **R0** and **R1**, stores the result back in **R0**, and then returns to the caller using the `BX LR` instruction.

2. Declare the Assembly Procedure in C

In our C code, we need to declare the assembly procedure as an external function using the **extern** keyword. This tells the C compiler that the function is implemented externally, in assembly.
Below (**Listing 2**) is the C code (**main.c**) that calls procedure **add_two_numbers**.

Listing 2.

```c
#include <stdio.h>

// Declare the assembly function
extern int add_two_numbers(int a, int b);

int main() {
    int result = add_two_numbers(5, 7);
    printf("Result: %d\n", result);
    return 0;
}
```

Here, the **add_two_numbers** function is declared as an external function that takes two int arguments and returns an integer number.

3. Compile the Assembly and C Code

We need to compile the assembly code and the C code separately or together, depending on our toolchain and build system. We need to link the resulting object files together to create the final executable.
Example using GCC:

```
arm-none-eabi-gcc -c add_two_numbers.s -o add_two_numbers.o
arm-none-eabi-gcc -c main.c -o main.o
arm-none-eabi-gcc main.o add_two_numbers.o -o main.elf
```

This series of commands compiles the assembly file and C file into object files and then links them into a final executable (**main.elf**).

4. Follow ARM Calling Conventions

Ensure that your assembly code follows the ARM calling conventions:
- **Argument Passing**: The first four arguments to a function are passed in registers **R0** to **R3**. Additional arguments are passed on the stack.
- **Return Value**: The return value is passed back to the caller in register **R0**.
- **Stack Frame**: If your assembly procedure needs to use registers **R4** to **R11**, or the link register **LR**, you should push these onto the stack at the beginning of the procedure and pop them back before returning.

5. Linking and Running

Once compiled and linked, the program can be run on the target ARM platform. The C code will call the ARM assembly procedure as if it were any other C function.

6. Handling Stack and Local Variables

If your assembly procedure uses local variables, it should allocate space on the stack. The stack pointer (**SP**) should be adjusted accordingly at the start and end of the procedure.
Below (**Listing 3**) is the example of using local variables.

Listing 3.

```
.global add_three_numbers
add_three_numbers:
    PUSH {R4, LR}      // Save R4 and LR (link register)
    ADD  R4, R0, R1    // R4 = R0 + R1
    ADD  R0, R4, R2    // R0 = R4 + R2
    POP  {R4, LR}      // Restore R4 and LR
    BX   LR            // Return to caller
```

7. Error Handling and Debugging

While interfacing, ensure proper error handling by checking the return values of assembly procedures. Use debugging tools like GDB to step through the C and assembly code to ensure everything works as expected.

Processing integers

This section includes examples that illustrate the operations with integers using ARM assembly functions.

Example 1

In this example, the assembly function **add2** (**Listing 1**) performs the addition of two integers, returning the sum. The calling convention expects the two input parameters in the registers **r0** and **r1**, and the result is returned in **r0**.

Listing 1.

```
.syntax unified
.cpu cortex-m4
.thumb
.global add2
.section .text
add2:
    add r0, r1
    bx lr
```

Code Analysis:
1. **.syntax unified**: This specifies the use of the `unified` assembly syntax, which allows for a uniform way to write both ARM and Thumb instructions.
2. **.cpu cortex-m4**: Indicates that the code is written for the Cortex-M4 CPU, using its instruction set.
3. **.thumb**: Switches the processor to Thumb state, meaning it will use the 16-bit or mixed 16/32-bit instruction set instead of the full 32-bit ARM instruction set.
4. **.global add2**: Declares the **add2** function as globally accessible, meaning other code can call it.
5. **.section .text**: Places the function code in the `.text` section, where executable code resides.
6. **add2:** The label of the function, allowing it to be referenced elsewhere (e.g., by other functions or external code).

7. **add r0, r1**: This instruction adds the value in register **r1** to the value in register **r0**. The result is stored back in **r0**, which is a common way to return a result in ARM assembly (since **r0** is used for returning values).
8. **bx lr**: This instruction branches to the address in the link register (**lr**), which is the return address. This is effectively how the function returns to the caller.

The C code that calls this function looks like the following (**Listing 2**).

Listing 2.

```
#include <stdio.h>
extern int add2(int i1, int i2);

int main()
{
  int result = add2(-23, 90);
  printf("Result: %d\n", result);
  return 0;
}
```

The application produces the following output:

Result: 67

Example 2

We can modify the **add2** assembly function to use the addresses of the variables (pointers) as parameters. This can be done using the `ldr `(load register) instruction to load the values from the addresses passed as parameters.
The modified assembly code is shown in **Listing 3**.

Listing 3.

```
.syntax unified
.cpu cortex-m4
.thumb
.global add2
```

```
.section .text
add2:
    ldr r2, [r0]      // Load the value at the address in r0 into r2
    ldr r3, [r1]      // Load the value at the address in r1 into r3
    add r2, r2, r3    // Add the values in r2 and r3, store the result in r2
    mov r0, r2        // Move the result to register r0
    bx lr             // Return to the caller
```

Explanation of Changes:

1. **ldr r2, [r0]**: This instruction loads the value from the memory address stored in **r0** into register **r2**. In this case, **r0** is expected to hold the address of the first variable.
2. **ldr r3, [r1]**: Similarly, this instruction loads the value from the memory address stored in **r1** into register **r3**. **r1** is expected to hold the address of the second variable.
3. **add r2, r2, r3**: The values loaded into **r2** and **r3** are added together, and the result is stored in **r2**.
4. **mov r0, r2**: The result of the addition is moved to the register **r0**.

The C code that calls this function now looks like the following (**Listing 4**).

Listing 4.

```
#include <stdio.h>

extern int add2(int *i1, int *i2);

int main()
{
  int i1 = 39, i2 = -45;
  int result = add2(&i1, &i2);
  printf("Result: %d\n", result);
  return 0;
}
```

The application's output will then be:

Result: -6

Example 3

If an assembly function should return the address of a result to a C caller, we can use the following code (**Listing 5**).

Listing 5.

```
.syntax unified
.cpu cortex-m4
.thumb
.global add2
.section .text
add2:
    ldr r2, [r0]      // Load the value at the address in r0 into r2
    ldr r3, [r1]      // Load the value at the address in r1 into r3
    add r2, r2, r3    // Add the values in r2 and r3, store the result in r2
    str r2, [r0]      // Store the result back at the address in r0
    bx lr             // Return to the caller
```

In this code, the result of the addition is stored back into the memory address pointed to by **r0**, which effectively updates the value at the original address of the first variable. This operation is performed by the instruction

str r2, [r0]

The C caller now looks like the following (**Listing 6**).

Listing 6.

```
#include <stdio.h>
extern int* add2(int *i1, int *i2);

int main()
{
    int i1 = -111, i2 = -52;
    int result = *(add2(&i1, &i2));
    printf("Result: %d\n", result);
    return 0;
}
```

The application produces the following output:

Result: -163

Example 4

In this example, the ARM assembly function (**Listing 7**) subtracts two integers and then multiplies the result by a third integer. The function takes three parameters in registers **r0, r1,** and **r2**:

- **r0**: First integer.
- **r1**: Second integer.
- **r2**: Third integer (used for multiplication).

The result is stored in **r0**, which is returned to the caller.

Listing 7.

```
.syntax unified
.cpu cortex-m4
.thumb
.global sub_mul
.section .text
sub_mul:
    sub r0, r0, r1   // r0 = r0 - r1 (subtract the second integer from the first)
    mul r0, r0, r2   // r0 = r0 * r2 (multiply the result by the third integer)
    bx lr            // Return to the caller
```

Explanation of the Instructions:

- **sub r0, r0, r1**: This subtracts the value in **r1** from the value in **r0** and stores the result back in **r0**.
- **mul r0, r0, r2**: This multiplies the result of the subtraction (stored in **r0**) by the value in **r2** and stores the final result back in **r0**.
- **bx lr**: This instruction returns to the caller by branching to the address stored in the link register (**lr**).

The C code that calls the assembly function **sub_mul** is shown in **Listing 8**.

Listing 8.

```
#include <stdio.h>
extern int sub_mul(int i1, int i2, int i3);

int main()
{
  int result = sub_mul(-12, 9, 4);
  printf("Result = %d\n", result);
  return 0;
}
```

The application produces the following output:

Result = -84

Example 5

This example illustrates how to use an integer value declared in the assembly function **sub_mul** (**Listing 9**).

Listing 9.

```
.syntax unified
.cpu cortex-m4
.thumb
.global sub_mul
.section .data
      c1: .int 10
.section .text
sub_mul:
    sub r0, r0, r1
    ldr r2, =c1
    ldr r2, [r2]
    mul r0, r0, r2
    bx lr
```

In this function we defined the section `.data` using the directive

.section .data

This indicates the start of the `.data` section where variables or constants are stored in memory. In this case, **c1** is declared in this section. Here

c1: .int 10

declares an integer constant **c1** with the value 10 in the `.data` section. This value is stored in memory.

Inside the Function:

- **sub r0, r0, r1**: This subtracts the value in register **r1** from the value in register **r0**, and stores the result in **r0**.
- **ldr r2, =c1**: This loads the address of the constant **c1** into register **r2**. **c1** is a memory location that holds the value 10, and this instruction doesn't load the value yet—just the address.
- **ldr r2, [r2]**: This loads the value from the address stored in **r2** (which is the address of **c1**). Since **c1** contains 10, after this instruction, **r2** will hold the value 10.
- **mul r0, r0, r2**: This multiplies the value in **r0** (result of the subtraction) by the value in **r2** (which now holds 10).
- **bx lr**: This is a branch and exchange instruction that jumps back to the return address stored in the link register (**lr**). This effectively ends the function and returns control to the caller.

Summary of What the Function Does:

1. The function subtracts the second parameter (**r1**) from the first parameter (**r0**).
2. It loads the constant **c1** (which is 10) from memory.
3. It multiplies the result of the subtraction by 10.
4. The final result is stored in **r0** and returned to the caller.

The C code that calls the assembly function looks like the following (**Listing 10**).

Listing 10.

```
#include <stdio.h>
extern int sub_mul(int i1, int i2);

int main()
```

```
{
  int result = sub_mul(-12, 9);
  printf("Result = %d\n", result);
  return 0;
}
```

The application produces the following result:

Result = -210

Example 6

The assembly function **sub_mul** (**Listing 11**) illustrates how to save the result inside the `.data` section.

Listing 11.

```
.syntax unified
.cpu cortex-m4
.thumb
.global sub_mul
.section .data
    c1: .int 10
    res: .int 0
.section .text
sub_mul:
    sub r0, r0, r1
    ldr r2, =c1
    ldr r2, [r2]
    mul r3, r0, r2
    ldr r1, =res
    str r3, [r1]
    mov r0, r1
    bx lr
```

Here, `.section .data` declares the start of the data section, where variables and constants reside. In this section:
- **c1: .int 10**: Defines a constant **c1** with the value 10 in the **.data** section.

- **res: .int 0**: Defines memory location **res** initialized to 0. This will be used to store the result of the multiplication.

Inside the Function:

1. **sub r0, r0, r1**: This subtracts the value in **r1** from the value in **r0** and stores the result back into **r0**.
2. **ldr r2, =c1**: Loads the address of the constant **c1** into register **r2**. This does not load the value of **c1** yet—just the memory address where **c1** is stored.
3. **ldr r2, [r2]**: Loads the value stored at the address in **r2** (which is the value of **c1**). Since **c1** is defined as 10, this instruction loads 10 into **r2**.
4. **mul r3, r0, r2**: Multiplies the value in **r0** (result of the subtraction) by **r2** (which holds 10 after loading **c1**).
5. **ldr r1, =res**: Loads the address of the **res** variable (which is defined in the **.data** section) into **r1**. This prepares **r1** to store the result of the multiplication.
6. **str r3, [r1]**: Stores the value in **r3** (result of the multiplication) into the memory address pointed to by **r1** (which is the address of **res**).
7. **mov r0, r1**: Moves the value of **r1** (which holds the address of **res**) into **r0**. This means that **r0** now contains the address of the **res** variable, not the result itself.
8. **bx lr**: This is a branch and exchange instruction that returns to the caller by jumping to the address stored in the link register (**lr**), ending the function.

Summary of What the Function Does:

- The function takes two input parameters (**r0** and **r1**).
- It subtracts **r1** from **r0** and stores the result in **r0**.
- It multiplies this result by the constant **c1** (which is 10).
- The result of the multiplication is stored in the memory location res.
- The function returns the address of the **res** variable (where the result is stored), not the result itself.

The C code that calls the assembly function is shown in **Listing 12**.

Listing 12.

#include <stdio.h>

```c
extern int* sub_mul(int i1, int i2);

int main()
{
  printf("Result = %d\n", *(sub_mul(-11, -2)));
  return 0;
}
```

The application produces the following output:

Result = -90

Example 7

In this example, the assembly function **sub_div** (**Listing 13**) implements the operation $(a - b)/k$.

Listing 13.

```
.syntax unified
.cpu cortex-m4
.thumb
.global sub_div
.section .text
sub_div:
  b  next
k: .int 2
next:
  ldr r0, [r0]
  ldr r1, [r1]
  sub r0, r1
  ldr r2, =k
  ldr r2, [r2]
  sdiv r0, r0, r2
  bx  lr
```

Explanation

- **b next**: This instruction is an unconditional branch to the label **next**. This skips the **k:** label for now. The use of this branch ensures that **k:** is defined but not executed immediately when entering the function.
- **k: .int 2**: This defines a data label **k**, which stores the integer value 2 at a specific memory location. This value will be used later in the division operation.
- **next**: This label marks the next part of the function, where the actual computation begins.
- **ldr r0, [r0]**: This instruction loads the value stored at the memory address pointed to by **r0** into register **r0**. In a typical use case, **r0** would be passed in as a pointer to a variable, and this instruction retrieves the value stored at that address.
- **ldr r1, [r1]**: This instruction does the same as above but for the **r1** register, i.e., it loads the value from the memory address pointed to by **r1** into **r1**.
- **sub r0, r1**: This instruction subtracts the value in **r1** from the value in **r0**, storing the result back in **r0**.
- **ldr r2, =k**: This instruction loads the address of the label **k** into register **r2**.
- **ldr r2, [r2]**: This instruction loads the value stored at the address in **r2** (which is **k**) into **r2**. Since **k** holds the value 2, **r2** is now set to 2.
- **sdiv r0, r0, r2**: This performs signed division, dividing the value in **r0** (the result of **r0** - **r1**) by the value in **r2** (which is 2), storing the quotient in **r0**.
- **bx lr**: This instruction returns from the function by branching to the link register (**lr**), which holds the return address.

Summary:
This function performs the following operations:
1. It loads two values from the memory addresses stored in **r0** and **r1**.
2. It subtracts the value from **r1** from the value in **r0**.
3. It divides the result of the subtraction by 2 (using the value stored in **k**).
4. Finally, it returns the result in **r0**.

The **k: .int 2** section defines a constant 2, which is loaded and used for the division.
The C code that calls this assembly function is shown below (**Listing 14**).

Listing 14.

```
#include <stdio.h>
extern int sub_div(int *a, int *b); // (a-b)/k

int main()
{
  int a = 719, b = 11;
  int result = sub_div(&a, &b);
  printf("Result = %d\n", result);
  return 0;
}
```

The application produces the following output:

Result = 354

Example 8

Here is one more example of division where the assembly function **signed_div** calculates the result using the formula **(a+b)/(a-b)**. The function takes the parameter `a` in **r0** and parameter `b` in **r1**. The source code of the function is shown in **Listing 15**.

Listing 15.

```
.syntax unified
.cpu cortex-m4
.thumb
.global signed_div
.section .text
signed_div:
    subs   r2, r0, r1      // r2 = a - b
    beq    div_by_zero     // if (a - b) == 0, branch to div_by_zero
    adds   r0, r0, r1      // r0 = a + b
    sdiv   r0, r0, r2      // r0 = (a + b) / (a - b)
    bx     lr              // return result in r0
div_by_zero:
```

```
movs   r0, #-1          // return -1 if (a - b) == 0
bx     lr               // return result in r0
```

Explanation:
1. **subs r2, r0, r1**: Subtract **b** from **a** and store the result in **r2** (a - b).
2. **beq div_by_zero**: If **r2** is zero (a - b == 0), branch to **div_by_zero**.
3. **adds r0, r0, r1**: Add **a** and **b** and store the result in **r0** (a + b).
4. **sdiv r0, r0, r2**: Divide (a + b) by (a - b) and store the result in **r0**.
5. **bx lr**: Return from the function.
6. **div_by_zero**: If (a - b) == 0, set **r0** to -1 and return.

The C code that calls the function **signed_div** looks like the following (**Listing 16**).

Listing 16.

```
#include <stdio.h>
extern int signed_div(int a, int b); // (a-b)/k

int main()
{
  int a = 71, b = 11;
  int result = signed_div(a, b);
  if (result == -1)
    printf("Divide by zero.\n");
  else
    printf("Result = %d\n", result);
  return 0;
}
```

The application produces the following output:

Result = 1

Example 9

In ARM architecture, the result of a division operation using `SDIV` or `UDIV` is stored directly in the destination register (Rd). There isn't a separate `reminder` or remainder register for division. If we need the remainder of a division, we would typically use additional instructions to calculate it.

Calculating the Remainder

To find the remainder of a division, we can use the following approach:
1. Perform the division to get the quotient.
2. Multiply the quotient by the divisor.
3. Subtract this product from the original dividend.

Here's an example in ARM assembly:

```
UDIV R0, R1, R2   // R0 = R1 / R2 (quotient)
MUL  R3, R0, R2   // R3 = R0 * R2 (product)
SUB  R4, R1, R3   // R4 = R1 - R3 (remainder)
```

The following assembly function **calculate_reminder** (**Listing 17**) calculates the remainder of division of two unsigned integers.

Listing 17.

```
.syntax unified
.cpu cortex-m4
.thumb
.global calculate_reminder
.section .text
calculate_reminder:
    udiv r2, r0, r1    // r2 = r0 / r1 (quotient)
    mul  r3, r1, r2    // r3 = r1 * r2 (product)
    sub  r4, r0, r3    // r4 = r0 - r3 (remainder)
    mov  r0, r4        // return -reminder
    bx   lr            // return result in r0
```

Code Breakdown:
1. **udiv r2, r0, r1**: Performs an unsigned division: **r2 = r0 / r1**. **r0** holds the dividend (numerator). **r1** holds the divisor (denominator). The quotient is stored in **r2**.

2. **mul r3, r1, r2**: Performs a multiplication: **r3** = **r1** * **r2**. This multiplies the divisor (**r1**) by the quotient (**r2**), producing the value of the largest multiple of **r1** that is less than or equal to **r0**.
3. **sub r4, r0, r3**: Subtracts the product (**r3**) from the original dividend (**r0**): **r4** = **r0** - **r3**. This operation gives the remainder of the division (**r0** % **r1**), since **r0** = (**r1** * quotient) + remainder.
4. **mov r0, r4**: Moves the remainder (**r4**) into **r0** to store the final result in the return register.
5. **bx lr**: Branches back to the calling function by returning from the function (using the link register **lr**).

Functionality Summary:

This function calculates the remainder of the unsigned division **r0** % **r1**:
1. **Inputs**:
   - **r0**: Dividend.
   - **r1**: Divisor.
2. **Output**: The remainder of **r0** / **r1** is returned in **r0**.

The C code that calls the assembly function **calculate_reminder** is shown in **Listing 18**.

Listing 18.

```
#include <stdio.h>

extern int calculate_reminder(int a, int b); // (a-b)/k

int main()
{
  int a = 20, b = 7;
  int result = calculate_reminder(a, b);
  printf("Reminder = %d\n", result);
  return 0;
}
```

The application produces the following output:

Reminder = 6

Example 10

Here is an ARM assembly function **find_max** (**Listing 19**) for the Cortex-M4 that searches for the maximum value in an integer array. The function takes two parameters: the address of the array in **r0** and the size of the array in **r1**. It returns the maximum value in **r0**.

Listing 19.

```
.syntax unified
.cpu cortex-m4
.thumb
.global find_max
.section .text
find_max:
    cmp    r1, #0              // Check if size is 0
    beq    array_empty         // If size is 0, return a default value (-1)
    ldr    r2, [r0], #4        // Load the first element of the array
                               //into r2 and increment r0
    subs   r1, r1, #1          // Decrease the size by 1
loop:
    cmp    r1, #0              // Check if we have reached the end of the array
    beq    done                // If r1 is 0, we are done
    ldr    r3, [r0], #4        // Load the next element of the array into r3 and
increment r0
    cmp    r3, r2              // Compare r3 (current element) with r2
                               // (current max)
    ble    skip_update         // If r3 <= r2, skip the update
    mov    r2, r3              // Update r2 with the new maximum value
skip_update:
    subs   r1, r1, #1          // Decrease the size counter
    b      loop                // Repeat the loop
done:
    mov    r0, r2              // Move the max value into r0 (return value)
    bx     lr                  // Return from the function
array_empty:
    mov    r0, #-1             // If the array is empty, return -1
                               //  as a default value
    bx     lr                  // Return from the function
```

Explanation:

1. **cmp r1, #0**: Check if the array size is 0. If so, branch to **array_empty**.
2. **ldr r2, [r0], #4**: Load the first element of the array into **r2** (the current maximum), and post-increment the address in **r0** by 4 (size of an integer).
3. **subs r1, r1, #1**: Decrement the array size by 1.
4. **loop**: The main loop starts here. It checks if the size counter **r1** has reached zero. If so, it branches to **done**.
5. **ldr r3, [r0], #4**: Load the next element of the array into **r3** and increment the pointer **r0** to point to the next element.
6. **cmp r3, r2**: Compare the current element (**r3**) with the current maximum (**r2**).
7. **ble skip_update**: If the current element is less than or equal to the maximum, skip updating the max.
8. **mov r2, r3**: If the current element is larger, update **r2** with the new maximum.
9. **b loop**: Continue looping through the array until all elements are processed.
10. **done**: After the loop, move the maximum value from **r2** to **r0** and return it.
11. **array_empty**: If the array size was 0, return -1 as a default value.

The C code that calls the assembly function **find_max** looks like the following (**Listing 20**).

Listing 20.

```
#include <stdio.h>

extern int find_max(int *a1, int asize);
int a1[5] = { -4, -6, -11, -2, -10 };

int main()
{
  int max_int = find_max(a1, 5);
  printf("Maximum = %d\n", max_int);
  return 0;
}
```

The application produces the following output:

Maximum = -2

Example 11

Because the ARM Thumb instruction set supports conditional execution with the IT-block, we can easily optimize the assembly function **find_max**. We can replace the instruction `ble skip_update` with `it gt`, which will execute the update of the maximum only if the current element is greater than the current maximum.
The modified version of **find_max** is shown in **Listing 21**.
Listing 21.

```
.syntax unified
.cpu cortex-m4
.thumb
.global find_max
.section .text
find_max:
    cmp    r1, #0        // Check if size is 0
    beq    array_empty   // If size is 0, return a default value (-1)
    ldr    r2, [r0], #4  // Load the first element of the array
                         // into r2 and increment r0
    subs   r1, r1, #1    // Decrease the size by 1
loop:
    cmp    r1, #0        // Check if we have reached the end of the array
    beq    done          // If r1 is 0, we are done
    ldr    r3, [r0], #4  // Load the next element of the
                         // array into r3 and increment r0
    cmp    r3, r2        // Compare r3 (current element)
                         // with r2 (current max)
    it     gt            // If r3 > r2, execute the following instruction
    movgt  r2, r3        // Update r2 with the new
                         //maximum value if r3 > r2
    subs   r1, r1, #1    // Decrease the size counter
    b      loop          // Repeat the loop
done:
    mov    r0, r2        // Move the max value into r0 (return value)
```

```
    bx    lr              // Return from the function
array_empty:
    mov   r0, #-1         // If the array is empty, return -1 as a default value
    bx    lr              // Return from the function
```

Explanation of the Optimization:

- **it gt**: This sets up the next instruction (**movgt r2, r3**) to execute only if the condition **gt** (greater than) is true based on the previous comparison (**cmp r3, r2**).

- **movgt r2, r3**: This moves the value of **r3** into **r2** (updating the maximum) only if **r3 > r2**.

This optimization reduces the need for a branch (**ble skip_update**) and makes the code more efficient by using the IT-block for conditional execution. It improves performance by avoiding the extra jump for each iteration where the condition **r3 <= r2** is true. It improves performance by avoiding the extra jump for each iteration where the condition **r3 <= r2** is true.

Example 12

It is easily to modify the assembly function **find_max** from **Example 11** in order to find the minimum value. The assembly function named **find_min** is shown in **Listing 22**.

Listing 22.

```
.syntax unified
.cpu cortex-m4
.thumb
.global find_min
.section .text
find_min:
    cmp    r1, #0          // Check if size is 0
    beq    array_empty     // If size is 0, return a default value (-1)
    ldr    r2, [r0], #4    // Load the first element of
                           // the array into r2 and increment r0
    subs   r1, r1, #1      // Decrease the size by 1
```

```
loop:
    cmp    r1, #0         // Check if we have reached the end of the array
    beq    done           // If r1 is 0, we are done

    ldr    r3, [r0], #4   // Load the next element of
                          // the array into r3 and increment r0
    cmp    r3, r2         // Compare r3 (current element) with r2
                          // (current min)
    it     lt             // If r3 < r2, execute the following instruction
    movlt  r2, r3         // Update r2 with the new minimum
                          //value if r3 < r2

    subs   r1, r1, #1     // Decrease the size counter
    b      loop           // Repeat the loop
done:
    mov    r0, r2         // Move the min value into r0 (return value)
    bx     lr             // Return from the function

array_empty:
    mov    r0, #-1        // If the array is empty, return -1 as a default value
    bx     lr             // Return from the function
```

Changes Made:
1. **cmp r3, r2:** This compares the current element (**r3**) with the current minimum (**r2**).
2. **it lt:** The IT-block is set to conditionally execute the following instruction if **r3** is less than (**lt**) **r2**.
3. **movlt r2, r3:** This moves the value of **r3** into **r2** (updating the minimum) only if **r3** is less than **r2**.

Example 13

We can modify the assembly function **find_min** from **Example 12** to return the **index** of the minimum value rather than the value itself. To do that, we need to track the index during the iteration. Here's the modified ARM assembly function named **find_min_index** (**Listing 23**) that finds the **index** of the minimum value in an integer array:

Listing 23.

```
.syntax unified
.cpu cortex-m4
.thumb
.global find_min_index
.section .text
find_min_index:
    cmp     r1, #0          // Check if size is 0
    beq     array_empty     // If size is 0, return -1

    mov     r3, #0          // Initialize index counter (r3 = current index)
    mov     r4, #0          // Initialize min_index to 0 (store min index in r4)

    ldr     r2, [r0], #4    // Load the first element of the array
                            // into r2 and increment r0
    subs    r1, r1, #1      // Decrease the size by 1

loop:
    cmp     r1, #0          // Check if we have reached the end of the array
    beq     done            // If r1 is 0, we are done

    add     r3, r3, #1      // Increment index counter (r3 = current index)
    ldr     r5, [r0], #4    // Load the next element of the array
                            //into r5 and increment r0
    cmp     r5, r2          // Compare r5 (current element) with
                            // r2 (current min)
    it      lt              // If r5 < r2, execute the following instruction
    movlt   r2, r5          // Update r2 with the new minimum value if r5 < r2
    it      lt              // If r5 < r2, execute the following instruction
    movlt   r4, r3          // Update r4 with the index of the new minimum

    subs    r1, r1, #1      // Decrease the size counter
    b       loop            // Repeat the loop

done:
    mov     r0, r4          // Move the index of the min value
                            // into r0 (return value)
    bx      lr              // Return from the function

array_empty:
```

```
    mov    r0, #-1      // If the array is empty, return -1
    bx     lr           // Return from the function
```

Changes Made:
1. **mov r3, #0**: This initializes **r3** as an index counter to track the current index.
2. **mov r4, #0**: This initializes **r4** to store the index of the current minimum, starting at 0.
3. **add r3, r3, #1**: This increments the index counter after each iteration.
4. **movlt r4, r3**: If a new minimum value is found, the current index (**r3**) is stored in **r4** as the new minimum index.
5. At the end of the loop: The function returns the index of the minimum value in **r0**.

Explanation:
- The function initializes the index of the minimum (**r4**) to 0 and iterates through the array.
- For each element, it compares it to the current minimum.
- If a smaller element is found, it updates both the minimum value and its index.
- Finally, the function returns the index of the minimum element. If the array is empty, it returns -1.

Example 14

In order to get the index of maximum in the array, the assembly function **find_max_index** may come in handy (**Listing 24**).

Listing 24.

```
.syntax unified
.cpu cortex-m4
.thumb
.global find_max_index
.section .text
find_max_index:
    cmp    r1, #0        // Check if size is 0
    beq    array_empty   // If size is 0, return -1
```

```
mov    r3, #0        // Initialize index counter (r3 = current index)
mov    r4, #0        // Initialize min_index to 0 (store min index in r4)

ldr    r2, [r0], #4  // Load the first element of the array
                     // into r2 and increment r0
subs   r1, r1, #1    // Decrease the size by 1

loop:
  cmp    r1, #0        // Check if we have reached the end of the array
  beq    done          // If r1 is 0, we are done
  add    r3, r3, #1    // Increment index counter (r3 = current index)
  ldr    r5, [r0], #4  // Load the next element of the
                       //array into r5 and increment r0
  cmp    r5, r2        // Compare r5 (current element) with r2
                       //(current min)
  it     gt            // If r5 > r2, execute the following instruction
  movgt  r2, r5        // Update r2 with the new minimum value if r5 < r2
  it     gt            // If r5 > r2, execute the following instruction
  movgt  r4, r3        // Update r4 with the index of the new minimum
  subs   r1, r1, #1    // Decrease the size counter
  b      loop          // Repeat the loop
done:
  mov    r0, r4        // Move the index of the min value
                       //into r0 (return value)
  bx     lr            // Return from the function
array_empty:
  mov    r0, #-1       // If the array is empty, return -1
  bx     lr            // Return from the function
```

The C code that calls the **find_max_index** is shown in **Listing 25**.

Listing 25.

```
#include <stdio.h>

extern int find_max_index(int *a1, int asize);
int a1[5] = { -74, -6, -11, -132, -2 };

int main()
```

```c
{
    int max_ind = find_max_index(a1, 5);
    printf("Index of Maximum = %d\n", max_ind);
    return 0;
}
```

The application produces the following output:

Index of Maximum = 4

Example 15

In this example, the assembly function **count_negatives** (**Listing 26**) counts the number of negative elements in an integer array. The function takes two parameters, the address of an array (**r0**) and its size (**r1**).

Listing 26.

```
.syntax unified
.cpu cortex-m4
.thumb
.global count_negatives
.section .text
count_negatives:
        cmp     r1, #0      // Check if array size is 0
        beq     done        // If size is 0, return 0 (r0 = 0)
        mov     r2, #0      // Initialize counter for negative elements (r2 = 0)
        mov     r3, r0      // Copy base address of the array to r3
loop:
        ldr     r4, [r3], #4    // Load the next element of the array into r4
                            // and update r3 to point to the next element
        cmp     r4, #0          // Compare the element with 0
        blt     increment_counter   // If the element is negative,
                            // increment the counter
next_element:
        subs    r1, r1, #1  // Decrease the size counter (r1 = r1 - 1)
        bne     loop        // If there are more elements, continue looping
done:
        mov     r0, r2  // Move the result (count of negative elements) to r0
```

```
        bx    lr          // Return to caller
increment_counter:
        add    r2, r2, #1     // Increment the counter for negative elements
        b      next_element  // Go to next element
```

Explanation:

1. **Function Parameters**:
    - **r0**: The base address of the array.
    - **r1**: The size of the array (number of elements).
2. **Initialization**:
    - **r2** is initialized to 0 to hold the count of negative elements.
    - **r3** is used to iterate through the array, holding the current address of the element being checked.
3. **Looping**:
    - The `ldr` instruction loads each element of the array into register **r4**, and the array pointer (**r3**) is updated after each load by incrementing by 4 (since each integer is 4 bytes).
    - The `cmp` instruction checks if the loaded element is negative. If the element is negative (**r4** < 0), the program branches to **increment_counter** to increment the counter **r2**.
4. **Completion**:
    - The loop continues until all elements are processed, at which point the counter **r2** (holding the number of negative elements) is moved to **r0**, and the function returns to the caller.

The C code that calls the function **count_negatives** looks like the following (**Listing 27**).

Listing 27.

```c
#include <stdio.h>

extern int count_negatives(int *a1, int asize);
int a1[10] = { -74, -6, 11, 12, -2, 334, 9, -63, 77, -1 };

int main()
{
  int num_neg = count_negatives(a1, 10);
  printf("Number of negatives = %d\n", num_neg);
```

```
  return 0;
}
```

The application produces the following output:

Number of negatives = 5

Example 16

We can easily modify the assembly function **count_negatives** to count the positive elements. The modified function named **count_positives** is shown in **Listing 28**.

Listing 28.

```
.syntax unified
.cpu cortex-m4
.thumb
.global count_positives
.section .text
count_positives:
      cmp    r1, #0        // Check if array size is 0
      beq    done          // If size is 0, return 0 (r0 = 0)

      mov    r2, #0     // Initialize counter for positive elements (r2 = 0)
      mov    r3, r0     // Copy base address of the array to r3
loop:
      ldr   r4, [r3], #4   // Load the next element of the array into r4 and
                          // update r3 to point to the next element
      cmp   r4, #0       // Compare the element with 0
      bgt   increment_counter  // If the element is positive,
                              // increment the counter
next_element:
      subs   r1, r1, #1 // Decrease the size counter (r1 = r1 - 1)
      bne    loop        // If there are more elements, continue looping
done:
      mov    r0, r2    // Move the result (count of positive elements) to r0
      bx     lr           // Return to caller
increment_counter:
      add    r2, r2, #1     // Increment the counter for positive elements
```

```
b      next_element   // Go to next element
```

Modifications:
1. Change the comparison condition:
    *   In the original **count_negatives** function, we used `blt` (branch if less than) to count negative numbers.
    *   In this modified version, we use `bgt` (branch if greater than) to count positive numbers.

Explanation of Changes:
*   The condition `cmp r4, #0` remains the same, as we're still comparing the current array element with zero.
*   The key difference is the branch instruction: now `bgt` checks if the value in **r4** is greater than zero (positive numbers). If it is, it branches to **increment_counter** to increase the counter for positive numbers.

After changes are made, the function will iterate through the array, counting the number of positive numbers and returning the count in **r0**.

The C code that calls **count_positives** is shown in **Listing 29**.

Listing 29.

```
#include <stdio.h>

extern int count_positives(int *a1, int asize);
int a1[10] = { 98, -46, 101, 12, -2, 334, 9, -63, 77, -1 };

int main()
{
  int num_pos = count_positives(a1, 10);
  printf("Number of positives = %d\n", num_pos);
  return 0;
}
```

The application produces the following output:

Number of positives = 6

Example 17

The ARM Thumb-2 instruction set allows for the use of the IT (If-Then) block, which can conditionally execute instructions without the need for branching. Using the IT block can optimize the function by reducing the number of branches, making the code more efficient and compact.

Here's (**Listing 30**) the optimized ARM assembly function **count_positives** for counting positive numbers using the IT conditional block:

Listing 30.

```
.syntax unified
.cpu cortex-m4
.global count_positives
.section .text
count_positives:
        cmp    r1, #0      // Check if array size is 0
        beq    done        // If size is 0, return 0 (r0 = 0)
        mov    r2, #0      // Initialize counter for positive elements (r2 = 0)
        mov    r3, r0      // Copy base address of the array to r3
loop:
        ldr    r4, [r3], #4    // Load the next element of the array into r4 and
                              // update r3 to point to the next element
        cmp    r4, #0      // Compare the element with 0
        it     gt          // Set up an IT block for "greater than"
        addgt  r2, r2, #1  // If r4 > 0, increment the counter
        subs   r1, r1, #1  // Decrease the size counter (r1 = r1 - 1)
        bne    loop        // If there are more elements, continue looping
done:
        mov    r0, r2      // Move the result (count of positive elements) to r0
        bx     lr          // Return to caller
```

Key Optimizations:
1. **IT Block:**
   - The `IT` instruction creates a conditional block that allows conditional execution of one or more instructions without the need for branching.

- The `it gt` block means that the instruction immediately following the IT (in this case, `addgt r2, r2, #1`) will only execute if the condition "greater than" (**gt**) is true, i.e., if **r4** > 0.
2. **Removing the Branch:**
   - In the previous version, we used a `bgt` instruction to branch if the element was positive. Now, the `addgt` instruction only executes when the element is positive, eliminating the need for the branch.

Explanation:

- The `cmp r4, #0` compares the current element (**r4**) with 0.
- The `it gt` sets up the condition to execute the next instruction only if **r4** is greater than 0.
- If the condition is true, the `addgt` instruction increments the counter **r2** (which holds the number of positive elements).
- The loop continues by decrementing **r1** (the size of the array) and checking if there are more elements to process.

Example 18

In this example, the assembly function **count_in_range** (**Listing 31**) calculates the number of array elements that are in range [-10, 10].

Listing 31.

```
.syntax unified
.cpu cortex-m4
.thumb
.global count_in_range
.section .text
count_in_range:
      push {lr}           // Save the link register
      mov  r2, #0         // r2 will store the count (initially 0)
      mov  r3, #-10       // r3 holds the lower bound (-10)
      mov  r4, #10        // r4 holds the upper bound (10)
loop:
      cmp  r1, #0         // Check if the size of the array is 0
      beq  done          // If size is 0, exit the loop
```

```
ldr  r5, [r0], #4     // Load the next element of the array into r5,
                      // increment r0
cmp  r5, r3           // Compare the element with the lower bound (-10)
blt  skip             // If the element is less than -10, skip
                      //to the next element
cmp  r5, r4           // Compare the element with the upper bound (10)
bgt  skip             // If the element is greater than 10, skip
                      // to the next element

add  r2, r2, #1       // If the element is in the range
                      // increment the count
skip:
subs r1, r1, #1       // Decrement the array size counter
bne  loop             // If there are more elements, repeat the loop
done:
mov  r0, r2           // Move the count to r0 (the return value)
pop  {lr}             // Restore the link register
bx   lr               // Return from the function
```

Explanation:

1. **Input parameters:**
   - **r0**: Address of the array.
   - **r1**: Size of the array.
2. **Output:**
   - **r0**: The number of elements within the range $[-10,10]$.

The function loops through the array, compares each element with -10 and 10, and increments the counter if the element falls within this range.

The C code that calls the **count_in_range** function is shown in **Listing 32**.

Listing 32.

```c
#include <stdio.h>

extern int count_in_range(int *a1, int asize);
int a1[10] = { -8, 46, -1, -12, 2, 3, 9, -63, 77, 1 };

int main()
{
  int count_rng = count_in_range(a1, 10);
```

```
    printf("Counted in range [-10, 10] : %d\n", count_rng);
    return 0;
}
```

The application produces the following output:

Counted in range [-10, 10] : 6

Example 19

Here's the modified version of the **count_in_range** function to count the
number of elements beyond the range [−10,10]. The logic is inverted to
count elements that are either less than −10 or greater than 10. The source
code of the function named **count_beyond_range** is shown in **Listing 33**.

Listing 33.

```
.syntax unified
.cpu cortex-m4
.thumb
.global count_beyond_range
.section .text
count_beyond_range:
        push {lr}          // Save the link register
        mov  r2, #0        // r2 will store the count (initially 0)
        mov  r3, #-10      // r3 holds the lower bound (-10)
        mov  r4, #10       // r4 holds the upper bound (10)

loop:
        cmp  r1, #0        // Check if the size of the array is 0
        beq  done          // If size is 0, exit the loop
        ldr  r5, [r0], #4  // Load the next element of the array into r5,
                           //increment r0
        cmp  r5, r3        // Compare the element with the
                           // lower bound (-10)
        blt  beyond        // If the element is less than -10,
                           // it is beyond the range
        cmp  r5, r4        // Compare the element with
                           // the upper bound (10)
```

```
        bgt  beyond        // If the element is greater than 10,
                           //it is beyond the range
        b    skip          // If the element is within the
                           //range, skip to the next element
beyond:
        add  r2, r2, #1     // If the element is beyond the
                           // range, increment the count
skip:
        subs r1, r1, #1     // Decrement the array size counter
        bne  loop          // If there are more elements, repeat the loop
done:
        mov  r0, r2         // Move the count to r0 (the return value)
        pop  {lr}           // Restore the link register
        bx   lr             // Return from the function
```

Explanation:

- The function now counts elements that are less than −10 (`blt beyond`) or greater than 10 (`bgt beyond`).
- If an element is within the range [−10,10], it is skipped (`b skip`), otherwise, it is counted (`add r2, r2, #1`).

The C code that calls the function **count_beyond_range** looks like the following (**Listing 34**).

Listing 34.

```
#include <stdio.h>

extern int count_beyond_range(int *a1, int asize);
int a1[10] = { -8, 46, -1, -12, 2, 3, 9, -63, 77, 1 };

int main()
{
  int count_beyond_rng = count_beyond_range(a1, 10);
  printf("Counted beyond range [-10, 10] : %d\n", count_beyond_rng);
  return 0;
}
```

The application produces the following output:

Example 20

This example illustrates how to optimize the **count_beyond_range** code. Below (**Listing 35**) is an optimized version of the **count_beyond_range** function using the IT (If-Then) block, which is available in ARM Thumb-2 instruction set. This reduces branching and makes the code more efficient.

Listing 35.

```
.syntax unified
.cpu cortex-m4
.thumb
.global count_beyond_range
.section .text
count_beyond_range:
        push {lr}           // Save the link register
        mov  r2, #0         // r2 will store the count (initially 0)
        mov  r3, #-10       // r3 holds the lower bound (-10)
        mov  r4, #10        // r4 holds the upper bound (10)

loop:
        cmp  r1, #0         // Check if the size of the array is 0
        beq  done          // If size is 0, exit the loop
        ldr  r5, [r0], #4   // Load the next element of
                            //the array into r5, increment r0
        cmp  r5, r3         // Compare the element
                            // with the lower bound (-10)
        it   lt            // If r5 is less than -10, execute the next instruction
        addlt r2, r2, #1    // Increment the count if r5 < -10
        cmp  r5, r4         // Compare the element with the upper bound (10)
        it   gt            // If r5 is greater than 10, execute
                            //the next instruction
        addgt r2, r2, #1    // Increment the count if r5 > 10
        subs r1, r1, #1     // Decrement the array size counter
        bne  loop          // If there are more
                            // elements, repeat the loop
done:
```

```
    mov  r0, r2        // Move the count to r0 (the return value)
    pop  {lr}          // Restore the link register
    bx   lr            // Return from the function
```

Optimizations:

IT block: The IT instruction (if-then) allows conditional execution of the subsequent instruction without the need for branching. Here, `lt` (less than) and `gt` (greater than) conditions are used with the IT block to increment the count when the array element is outside the range.

- `it lt` followed by `addlt r2, r2, #1` increments the count if the element is less than −10.
- `it gt` followed by `addgt r2, r2, #1` increments the count if the element is greater than 10.

This approach reduces the number of branches and improves code efficiency.

Example 21

In this example, an assembly function **reverse_sign** (**Listing 36**) reverses the sign of the elements in an integer array. The function takes two parameters: the address of the array in **r0** and the size of the array in **r1**. It loops through the array, negates each element, and updates the array.

Listing 36.

```
.syntax unified
.cpu cortex-m4
.thumb
.global reverse_sign
.section .text
reverse_sign:
    push   {r4, lr}      // Save r4 and return address
    cmp    r1, #0        // Compare size with 0
    beq    done          // If size is 0, return immediately
loop:
    ldr    r4, [r0], #4  // Load the current element,
                         // post-increment the pointer
    rsbs   r4, r4, #0    // Reverse sign (negate) using RSBS
```

```
str    r4, [r0, #-4]   // Store the negated value back to the array
subs   r1, r1, #1      // Decrement the size
bne    loop            // If size is not 0, continue loop
done:
pop    {r4, lr}        // Restore r4 and return address
bx     lr              // Return from function
```

Explanation:

- The function accepts the array address in **r0** and the array size in **r1**.
- The loop iterates over the array, loading each element, negating it using the `rsbs` instruction (which reverses the sign), and storing it back.
- The pointer in **r0** is incremented by 4 (the size of an integer) after each element is processed.
- The loop continues until all elements are processed.

The C code that calls this function is shown below (**Listing 37**).

Listing 37.

```
#include <stdio.h>

extern void reverse_sign(int *a1, int asize);
int a1[5] = { 23, -7, -85, 44, 6 };

int main()
{
  reverse_sign(a1, 5);
  printf("Updated array:\n");
  for (int i = 0; i < 5; i++)
    printf("%d ", a1[i]);
  return 0;
}
```

The application produces the following output:

Updated array:
-23 7 85 -44 -6

Example 22

Here's an assembly function **replace_negatives** (**Listing 38**) that replaces all negative elements with 0.

Listing 38.

```
.syntax unified
.cpu cortex-m4
.thumb
.global replace_negatives
.section .text
replace_negatives:
    push   {r4, lr}      // Save r4 and return address
    cmp    r1, #0        // Compare size with 0
    beq    done          // If size is 0, return immediately

loop:
    ldr    r4, [r0], #4   // Load the current element,
                          //post-increment the pointer
    cmp    r4, #0         // Compare the element with 0
    bge    next           // If the element is >= 0, skip to the next element
    mov    r4, #0         // If the element is negative, set it to 0
next:
    str    r4, [r0, #-4]  // Store the modified (or unmodified)
                          // value back to the array
    subs   r1, r1, #1     // Decrement the size
    bne    loop           // If size is not 0, continue loop
done:
    pop    {r4, lr}       // Restore r4 and return address
    bx     lr             // Return from function
```

Explanation:
- The function accepts the array address in **r0** and the array size in **r1**.
- Inside the loop, each element is loaded into **r4**.
- The `cmp` instruction checks if the element is negative (**r4** < 0). If it is, we replace the value with 0 (**mov r4, #0**).
- If the element is positive or zero, we skip the modification and store the original value.

- The loop continues until all elements are processed.

The C code that call the function **replace_negatives** is shown in **Listing 39**.

Listing 39.

```c
#include <stdio.h>
extern void replace_negatives(int *a1, int asize);
int a1[5] = { 23, -7, -85, 44, 6 };

int main()
{
  replace_negatives(a1, 5);
  printf("Updated array:\n");
  for (int i = 0; i < 5; i++)
    printf("%d  ", a1[i]);
  return 0;
}
```

The application produces the following output:

Updated array:
23 0 0 44 6

Example 23

It is easily to optimize the function **replace_negatives** using the IT-conditional block. The modified code of this function is shown in **Listing 40**.

Listing 40.

```
.syntax unified
.cpu cortex-m4
.thumb
.global replace_negatives
.section .text
replace_negatives:
```

```
    push   {r4, lr}      // Save r4 and return address
    cmp    r1, #0        // Compare size with 0
    beq    done          // If size is 0, return immediately
loop:
    ldr    r4, [r0], #4  // Load the current element,
                         // post-increment the pointer
    cmp    r4, #0        // Compare the element with 0
    it     lt
    movlt  r4, #0        // If the element is negative, set it to 0
    str    r4, [r0, #-4] // Store the modified (or unmodified)
                         // value back to the array
    subs   r1, r1, #1    // Decrement the size
    bne    loop          // If size is not 0, continue loop
done:
    pop    {r4, lr}      // Restore r4 and return address
    bx     lr            // Return from function
```

Explanation of Changes.

1. We remove the following sequence and label **next**:
```
    bge    next
    mov    r4, #0
next:
```
2. We then put the sequence
```
    it     lt
    movlt  r4, #0
```

Example 24

In order to replace all positive numbers of an integer array with 0, we should change the condition in the IT-block. The modified function named **replace_positives** will look like the following (**Listing 41**).

Listing 41.

```
.syntax unified
.cpu cortex-m4
.thumb
```

56

```
.global replace_positives
.section .text
replace_positives:
    push   {r4, lr}      // Save r4 and return address
    cmp    r1, #0        // Compare size with 0
    beq    done          // If size is 0, return immediately
loop:
    ldr    r4, [r0], #4  // Load the current element,
                         //post-increment the pointer
    cmp    r4, #0        // Compare the element with 0
    it     gt
    movgt  r4, #0        // If the element is positive, set it to 0

    str    r4, [r0, #-4] // Store the modified (or unmodified) value
                         // back to the array
    subs   r1, r1, #1    // Decrement the size
    bne    loop          // If size is not 0, continue loop
done:
    pop    {r4, lr}      // Restore r4 and return address
    bx     lr            // Return from function
```

The C code that calls the function **replace_positives** looks like the following (**Listing 42**).

Listing 42.

```c
#include <stdio.h>

extern void replace_positives(int *a1, int asize);
int a1[5] = { -23, 7, 85, -44, -6 };

int main()
{
  replace_positives(a1, 5);
  printf("Updated array:\n");
  for (int i = 0; i < 5; i++)
    printf("%d  ", a1[i]);
  return 0;
}
```

The application produces the following output:

Updated array:
-23 0 0 -44 -6

Example 25

Here is an assembly function **abs_array** (**Listing 43**) that calculates the absolute value of the elements of an integer array. The function takes two parameters: the address of the array in **r0** and the size of the array in **r1**. It processes each element, making negative values positive.

Listing 43.

```
.syntax unified
.cpu cortex-m4
.thumb
.global abs_array
.section .text
abs_array:
    push   {r4, lr}      // Save r4 and return address
    cmp    r1, #0        // Compare size with 0
    beq    done          // If size is 0, return immediately
loop:
    ldr    r4, [r0], #4  // Load the current element,
                         // post-increment the pointer
    cmp    r4, #0        // Compare the element with 0
    bge    next          // If element is >= 0, skip to the next element
    rsbs   r4, r4, #0    // If the element is negative, reverse its
                         // sign (absolute value)
next:
    str    r4, [r0, #-4] // Store the modified (or unmodified) value
                         // back to the array
    subs   r1, r1, #1    // Decrement the size
    bne    loop          // If size is not 0, continue loop
done:
    pop    {r4, lr}      // Restore r4 and return address
    bx     lr            // Return from function
```

Explanation:

- The function accepts the array address in **r0** and the array size in **r1**.
- Inside the loop, the `ldr` instruction loads each element into **r4**.
- If the element is negative (**r4** < 0), the `rsbs` instruction reverses its sign to compute its absolute value.
- The result (either the unchanged positive number or the modified absolute value) is stored back into the array using `str`.
- The loop continues until all elements have been processed.

The C code that calls the function **abs_array** is shown in **Listing 44**.

Listing 44.

```
#include <stdio.h>

extern void abs_array(int *a1, int asize);
int a1[5] = { -23, 7, 85, -44, -6 };

int main()
{
  abs_array(a1, 5);
  printf("Updated array:\n");
  for (int i = 0; i < 5; i++)
     printf("%d ", a1[i]);
  return 0;
}
```

The application produces the following output:

Updated array:
23 7 85 44 6

Example 26

Below (**Listing 45**) is an optimized version of the function **abs_array** where the IT-block is used.

Listing 45.

```
.syntax unified
.cpu cortex-m4
.thumb
.global abs_array
.section .text
abs_array:
    push    {r4, lr}        // Save r4 and return address
    cmp     r1, #0          // Compare size with 0
    beq     done            // If size is 0, return immediately
loop:
    ldr     r4, [r0], #4    // Load the current element,
                            // post-increment the pointer
    cmp     r4, #0          // Compare the element with 0
    it      lt              // IT block for less than condition
    rsbslt  r4, r4, #0      // Reverse sign if r4 is negative (absolute value)
    str     r4, [r0, #-4]   // Store the absolute value back to the array
    subs    r1, r1, #1      // Decrement the size
    bne     loop            // If size is not 0, continue loop
done:
    pop     {r4, lr}        // Restore r4 and return address
    bx      lr              // Return from function
```

Explanation of Changes:

- The instruction `it lt` ensures that the next instruction (**rsbslt**) is only executed when **r4** is negative.
- **rsbslt** (Reverse Subtract with Carry if Less Than) negates **r4** only if the comparison shows that the element is negative.

This corrected version avoids the unnecessary conditional instruction block.

Example 27

Here (**Listing 46**) is an assembly function **reverse_array** that reverses the order of elements in an integer array. The function takes two parameters: the address of the array in **r0** and the size of the array in **r1**.

Listing 46.

```
.syntax unified
.cpu cortex-m4
.thumb
.global reverse_array
.section .text
reverse_array:
    push   {r4, r5, lr}          // Save r4, r5, and return address
    mov    r2, r0                 // r2 = start address (array base)
    add    r3, r0, r1, LSL #2     // r3 = end address (r0 + size * 4)
    subs   r3, r3, #4             // Move r3 to point to the last element
    cmp    r2, r3                 // Compare start and end
    bge    done                   // If r2 >= r3, we're done
loop:
    ldr    r4, [r2]     // Load the element from the start of the array
    ldr    r5, [r3]     // Load the element from the end of the array
    str    r4, [r3]     // Store start element at the end
    str    r5, [r2]     // Store end element at the start
    add    r2, r2, #4   // Move to the next element from the start
    subs   r3, r3, #4   // Move to the previous element from the end

    cmp    r2, r3       // Compare updated pointers
    blt    loop         // If r2 < r3, continue the loop
done:
    pop    {r4, r5, lr}  // Restore r4, r5, and return address
    bx     lr            // Return from function
```

Explanation:

- The function accepts the array address in **r0** and the size of the array in **r1**.
- **r2** is initialized as the starting address of the array, and **r3** is calculated as the last element's address.
- The loop iterates, swapping elements from the start and end of the array.
- The loop continues until the start pointer (**r2**) meets or passes the end pointer (**r3**), meaning the array is fully reversed.
- The elements are swapped using `ldr` to load and `str` to store values.

The C code that calls the function **reverse_array** looks like the following (**Listing 47**).

Listing 47.

```
#include <stdio.h>

extern void reverse_array(int *a1, int asize);
int a1[5] = { -23, -667, -85, 44, -6 };

int main()
{
  reverse_array(a1, 5);
  printf("Updated array:\n");
  for (int i = 0; i < 5; i++)
     printf("%d  ", a1[i]);
  return 0;
}
```

The application produces the following output:

Updated array:
-6 44 -85 -667 -23

Example 28

In this example, an ARM assembly function **bubble_sort** (**Listing 48**) performs bubble sort in ascending order on an integer array.
The function takes two parameters:
- **r0**: the address of the array.
- **r1**: the size of the array.

Listing 48.

```
.syntax unified
.arch armv7-a
.thumb
.global bubble_sort
```

```
.section .text
bubble_sort:
    push {r4-r9, lr}
    mov r4, r0        // r4 = array address
    mov r5, r1        // r5 = array size
    sub r5, r5, #1    // r5 = array size - 1 (for outer loop)
outer_loop:
    mov r6, #0        // r6 = swapped flag
    mov r7, #0        // r7 = inner loop counter
inner_loop:
    lsl r8, r7, #2    // r8 = r7 * 4 (index * 4 for word-aligned addressing)
    add r8, r4, r8    // r8 = address of current element
    ldr r2, [r8]      // r2 = current element
    ldr r3, [r8, #4]  // r3 = next element
    cmp r2, r3
    ble no_swap

    // Swap elements
    str r3, [r8]
    str r2, [r8, #4]
    mov r6, #1        // Set swapped flag

no_swap:
    add r7, r7, #1    // Increment inner loop counter
    cmp r7, r5
    blt inner_loop

    cmp r6, #0        // Check if any swaps occurred
    beq done          // If no swaps, array is sorted
    sub r5, r5, #1    // Decrement outer loop counter
    cmp r5, #0
    bgt outer_loop
done:
    pop {r4-r9, pc}
```

Here's a brief explanation of how the code works:

1. The function takes two parameters:
   - **r0**: the address of the array
   - **r1**: the size of the array
2. It uses two nested loops:

- The outer loop runs for (size - 1) iterations
- The inner loop compares adjacent elements and swaps them if they're in the wrong order
3. A flag (**r6**) is used to optimize the sorting process. If no swaps occur in an iteration of the outer loop, the array is already sorted, and the function exits.
4. The function uses word-aligned addressing, assuming each integer occupies 4 bytes.

The C code that calls the function **bubble_sort** looks like the following (**Listing 49**).

Listing 49.

```
#include <stdio.h>

extern void bubble_sort(int* a1, int asize);

int main() {
    int arr[] = {25, 3, 38, -4, 2, -17, -8, 1, 44, -7};
    int size = sizeof(arr) / sizeof(arr[0]);

    printf("Original array: ");
    for (int i = 0; i < size; i++)
        printf("%d ", arr[i]);
    bubble_sort(arr, size);
    // Print sorted array
    printf("\nUpdated array: ");
    for (int i = 0; i < size; i++)
        printf("%d ", arr[i]);
    printf("\n");
    return 0;
}
```

The application produces the following output:

Original array: 25 3 38 -4 2 -17 -8 1 44 -7
Updated array: -17 -8 -7 -4 1 2 3 25 38 44

Example 29

It is easily to change the **bubble_sort** function to sort the array in descending order. In order to do that, we need to modify the comparison logic. The updated function named **bubble_sort_des** is shown in **Listing 50**.

Listing 50.

```
.syntax unified
.arch armv7-a
.thumb
.global bubble_sort_des
.section .text
bubble_sort_des:
    push {r4-r9, lr}
    mov r4, r0      // r4 = array address
    mov r5, r1      // r5 = array size
    sub r5, r5, #1   // r5 = array size - 1 (for outer loop)
outer_loop:
    mov r6, #0      // r6 = swapped flag
    mov r7, #0      // r7 = inner loop counter

inner_loop:
    lsl r8, r7, #2       // r8 = r7 * 4 (index * 4 for word-aligned addressing)
    add r8, r4, r8       // r8 = address of current element
    ldr r2, [r8]         // r2 = current element
    ldr r3, [r8, #4]     // r3 = next element
    cmp r2, r3
    bge no_swap          // Change from ble to bge for descending order

    // Swap elements
    str r3, [r8]
    str r2, [r8, #4]
    mov r6, #1      // Set swapped flag
no_swap:
    add r7, r7, #1   // Increment inner loop counter
    cmp r7, r5
    blt inner_loop
```

```
    cmp r6, #0      // Check if any swaps occurred
    beq done        // If no swaps, array is sorted
    sub r5, r5, #1  // Decrement outer loop counter
    cmp r5, #0
    bgt outer_loop
done:
    pop {r4-r9, pc}
```

Explanation of Changes.

The main change to sort in descending order is in the comparison logic.
Here's what was modified:
1. The line `cmp r2, r3` remains the same, as we still want to compare
   the current element (**r2**) with the next element (**r3**).
2. The conditional branch instruction changed from `ble` (branch if
   less than or equal) to `bge` (branch if greater than or equal):

```
cmp r2, r3
bge no_swap    // Change from ble to bge for descending order
```

This change means that we only swap elements if the current element is less
than the next element, which results in a descending order sort.
All other parts of the function remain the same. This modification will now
sort the array in descending order (from highest to lowest value).

The C code that calls the **bubble_sort_des** function is shown in **Listing 51**.

Listing 51.

```
#include <stdio.h>

extern void bubble_sort_des(int* a1, int asize);

int main() {
    int arr[] = {25, 3, 38, -4, 2, -17, -8, 1, 44, -7};
    int size = sizeof(arr) / sizeof(arr[0]);

    printf("Original array: ");
    for (int i = 0; i < size; i++)
```

```c
        printf("%d ", arr[i]);
    bubble_sort_des(arr, size);
    // Print sorted array
    printf("\nUpdated array: ");
    for (int i = 0; i < size; i++)
        printf("%d ", arr[i]);
    printf("\n");
    return 0;
}
```

The application produces the following output:

Original array: 25 3 38 -4 2 -17 -8 1 44 -7
Updated array: 44 38 25 3 2 1 -4 -7 -8 -17

Example 30

In this example, we modify the **bubble_sort_des** function to select only positive elements, write them into a separate array, and then sort that new array in descending order. This will require some significant changes to the function **bubble_sort_des**.
Below (**Listing 52**) is an assembly function **sort_positive_descending** that sorts only positive elements of an array.

Listing 52.

```
.syntax unified
.arch armv7-a
.global sort_positive_descending
.section .text
sort_positive_descending:
    push {r4-r11, lr}
    mov r4, r0      // r4 = input array address
    mov r5, r1      // r5 = input array size
    mov r6, r2      // r6 = output array address
    mov r7, r3      // r7 = address to store output size
    mov r8, #0       // r8 = output array size (counter)

    // First pass: copy positive elements to output array
```

```
copy_loop:
    ldr r9, [r4], #4    // Load element from input array and increment pointer
    cmp r9, #0
    ble skip_element     // Skip if not positive
    str r9, [r6, r8, lsl #2]  // Store in output array
    add r8, r8, #1            // Increment output size
skip_element:
    subs r5, r5, #1
    bne copy_loop

    // Store the size of the output array
    str r8, [r7]

    // If output array is empty or has only one element, we're done
    cmp r8, #2
    blt done

    // Bubble sort the output array in descending order
    sub r5, r8, #1     // r5 = output size - 1 (for outer loop)

outer_loop:
    mov r9, #0        // r9 = swapped flag
    mov r10, #0       // r10 = inner loop counter

inner_loop:
    lsl r11, r10, #2
    add r11, r6, r11     // r11 = address of current element
    ldr r0, [r11]        // r0 = current element
    ldr r1, [r11, #4]    // r1 = next element
    cmp r0, r1
    bge no_swap          // If current >= next, no swap needed

    // Swap elements
    str r1, [r11]
    str r0, [r11, #4]
    mov r9, #1          // Set swapped flag

no_swap:
    add r10, r10, #1    // Increment inner loop counter
    cmp r10, r5
```

```
  blt inner_loop

  cmp r9, #0        // Check if any swaps occurred
  beq done          // If no swaps, array is sorted

  subs r5, r5, #1   // Decrement outer loop counter
  bne outer_loop
done:
  pop {r4-r11, pc}
```

This new function, **sort_positive_descending**, does the following:

1. It takes four parameters:
   - **r0**: address of the input array
   - **r1**: size of the input array
   - **r2**: address of the output array (where positive elements will be stored)
   - **r3**: address to store the size of the output array
2. It first copies only the positive elements from the input array to the output array, counting how many elements are copied.
3. It stores the count of positive elements (size of the output array) at the address provided in **r3**.
4. If the output array has fewer than 2 elements, it skips the sorting step.
5. It then performs **bubble_sort_des** on the output array, sorting the positive elements in descending order.

Key differences from the **bubble_sort_des** function:
- It handles two arrays: input and output.
- It filters for positive elements during the copying phase.
- The sorting phase only operates on the output array containing positive elements.
- The comparison for descending order is maintained (`bge` for "branch if greater than or equal").

The C code that calls the **sort_positive_descending** function is shown in **Listing 53**.

Listing 53.

```
#include <stdio.h>
extern void sort_positive_descending(int* iarr, int isize, int *oarr, int *osize);

int main() {
    int iarr[] = {25, 3, 38, -4, 2, -17, -8, 1, 44, -7};
    int isize = sizeof(iarr) / sizeof(iarr[0]);
    int oarr[10] = {0, 0, 0, 0, 0, 0, 0, 0, 0, 0};
    int osize = sizeof(oarr) / sizeof(oarr[0]);

    printf("Original array: ");
    for (int i = 0; i < isize; i++)
        printf("%d ", iarr[i]);
    sort_positive_descending(iarr, isize, oarr, &osize);
    // Print sorted array
    printf("\nUpdated array: ");
    for (int i = 0; i < osize; i++)
        printf("%d ", oarr[i]);
    printf("\n");
    return 0;
}
```

The application produces the following output:

Original array: 25 3 38 -4 2 -17 -8 1 44 -7
Updated array: 44 38 25 3 2 1

Example 31

This example illustrates how to modify the **sort_positive_descending**
function to sort the positive elements in ascending order instead. The main
change will be in the comparison logic during the sorting phase.
This new function, **sort_positive_ascending** (**Listing 54**) takes four
parameters:

- **r0**: address of the input array.
- **r1**: size of the input array.
- **r2**: address of the output array (where positive elements will be
  stored).
- **r3**: address to store the size of the output array.

Listing 54.

```
.syntax unified
.arch armv7-a
.global sort_positive_ascending
.section .text
sort_positive_ascending:
    push {r4-r11, lr}
    mov r4, r0        // r4 = input array address
    mov r5, r1        // r5 = input array size
    mov r6, r2        // r6 = output array address
    mov r7, r3        // r7 = address to store output size
    mov r8, #0        // r8 = output array size (counter)

    //First pass: copy positive elements to output array
copy_loop:
    ldr r9, [r4], #4   // Load element from input array and increment pointer
    cmp r9, #0
    ble skip_element   // Skip if not positive
    str r9, [r6, r8, lsl #2]  // Store in output array
    add r8, r8, #1            // Increment output size
skip_element:
    subs r5, r5, #1
    bne copy_loop

    // Store the size of the output array
    str r8, [r7]

    // If output array is empty or has only one element, we're done
    cmp r8, #2
    blt done

    // Bubble sort the output array in ascending order
    sub r5, r8, #1     // r5 = output size - 1 (for outer loop)
outer_loop:
    mov r9, #0         // r9 = swapped flag
    mov r10, #0        // r10 = inner loop counter
inner_loop:
    lsl r11, r10, #2
```

```
    add r11, r6, r11    // r11 = address of current element
    ldr r0, [r11]       // r0 = current element
    ldr r1, [r11, #4]   // r1 = next element

    cmp r0, r1
    ble no_swap         // If current <= next,
                        // no swap needed (changed from bge to ble)

    // Swap elements
    str r1, [r11]
    str r0, [r11, #4]
    mov r9, #1          // Set swapped flag
no_swap:
    add r10, r10, #1    // Increment inner loop counter
    cmp r10, r5
    blt inner_loop
    cmp r9, #0          // Check if any swaps occurred
    beq done            // If no swaps, array is sorted
    subs r5, r5, #1     // Decrement outer loop counter
    bne outer_loop
done:
    pop {r4-r11, pc}
```

The main change to sort in ascending order concerns the sorting phase, where the comparison logic has been modified:

```
cmp r0, r1
ble no_swap    //If current <= next, no swap
               //needed (changed from bge to ble)
```

All other parts of the function remain the same.

The C code that calls the **sort_positive_ascending** function is shown in **Listing 55**.

Listing 55.

```
#include <stdio.h>

extern void sort_positive_ascending(int* iarr, int isize, int *oarr, int *osize);
```

```
int main() {
    int iarr[] = {25, 3, 38, -4, 2, -17, -8, 1, 44, -7};
    int isize = sizeof(iarr) / sizeof(iarr[0]);
    int oarr[10] = {0, 0, 0, 0, 0, 0, 0, 0, 0, 0};
    int osize = sizeof(oarr) / sizeof(oarr[0]);

    printf("Original array: ");
    for (int i = 0; i < isize; i++)
        printf("%d ", iarr[i]);
    sort_positive_ascending(iarr, isize, oarr, &osize);
    // Print sorted array
    printf("\nUpdated array: ");
    for (int i = 0; i < osize; i++)
        printf("%d ", oarr[i]);
    printf("\n");
    return 0;
}
```

The application produces the following output:

Original array: 25 3 38 -4 2 -17 -8 1 44 -7
Updated array: 1 2 3 25 38 44

Example 32

This example illustrates how to sort the negative elements of an integer array in ascending order. We will modify the **sort_positive_ascending** function code in the following way:

1. The function name will be changed to **sort_negative_ascending** to reflect its new purpose.
2. In the copying phase, the condition for selecting elements has been changed

    cmp r9, #0
    bge skip_element // Skip if not negative
                    //(changed from ble to bge)
    This change means we now copy only negative elements to the output array.

3. The sorting logic remains the same as in the ascending order sort for positive numbers, because negative numbers in ascending order follow the same comparison logic (e.g., -5 < -3 < -1).

The source code of the function **sort_negative_ascending** is shown in **Listing 56.**

Listing 56.

```
.syntax unified
.arch armv7-a
.global sort_negative_ascending
.section .text
sort_negative_ascending:
    push {r4-r11, lr}
    mov r4, r0      // r4 = input array address
    mov r5, r1      // r5 = input array size
    mov r6, r2      // r6 = output array address
    mov r7, r3      // r7 = address to store output size
    mov r8, #0      // r8 = output array size (counter)

    // First pass: copy negative elements to output array
copy_loop:
    ldr r9, [r4], #4      // Load element from input
                         // array and increment pointer
    cmp r9, #0
    bge skip_element     // Skip if not negative (changed from ble to bge)
    str r9, [r6, r8, lsl #2]  // Store in output array
    add r8, r8, #1           // Increment output size
skip_element:
    subs r5, r5, #1
    bne copy_loop

    // Store the size of the output array
    str r8, [r7]

    // If output array is empty or has only one element, we're done
    cmp r8, #2
    blt done
```

```
// Bubble sort the output array in ascending order
sub r5, r8, #1      // r5 = output size - 1 (for outer loop)

outer_loop:
    mov r9, #0       // r9 = swapped flag
    mov r10, #0      // r10 = inner loop counter

inner_loop:
    lsl r11, r10, #2
    add r11, r6, r11  // r11 = address of current element
    ldr r0, [r11]     // r0 = current element
    ldr r1, [r11, #4] // r1 = next element

    cmp r0, r1
    ble no_swap       // If current <= next, no swap needed

    // Swap elements
    str r1, [r11]
    str r0, [r11, #4]
    mov r9, #1        // Set swapped flag

no_swap:
    add r10, r10, #1  // Increment inner loop counter
    cmp r10, r5
    blt inner_loop

    cmp r9, #0        // Check if any swaps occurred
    beq done          // If no swaps, array is sorted
    subs r5, r5, #1   // Decrement outer loop counter
    bne outer_loop
done:
    pop {r4-r11, pc}
```

The resulting output array will contain all negative elements from the input array, sorted in ascending order (from the most negative to the least negative).

The C code that calls the **sort_negative_ascending** function looks like the following (**Listing 57**).

Listing 57.

```c
#include <stdio.h>

extern void sort_negative_ascending(int* iarr, int isize, int *oarr, int *osize);

int main() {
    int iarr[] = {25, 3, 38, -4, 2, -17, -8, 1, 44, -7};
    int isize = sizeof(iarr) / sizeof(iarr[0]);
    int oarr[10] = {0, 0, 0, 0, 0, 0, 0, 0, 0, 0};
    int osize = sizeof(oarr) / sizeof(oarr[0]);

    printf("Original array: ");
    for (int i = 0; i < isize; i++)
        printf("%d ", iarr[i]);
    sort_negative_ascending(iarr, isize, oarr, &osize);
    // Print sorted array
    printf("\nUpdated array: ");
    for (int i = 0; i < osize; i++)
        printf("%d ", oarr[i]);
    printf("\n");
    return 0;
}
```

The application produces the following output:

Original array: 25 3 38 -4 2 -17 -8 1 44 -7
Updated array: -17 -8 -7 -4

Example 33

It's quite straightforward to modify the **sort_negative_ascending** function to create a **sort_negative_descending** version. The main change would be in the comparison logic during the sorting phase.
The code of **sort_negative_descending** is shown in **Listing 58**.

Listing 58.

.syntax unified

```
.arch armv7-a
.global sort_negative_descending
.section .text
sort_negative_descending:
    push {r4-r11, lr}
    mov r4, r0        // r4 = input array address
    mov r5, r1        // r5 = input array size
    mov r6, r2        // r6 = output array address
    mov r7, r3        // r7 = address to store output size
    mov r8, #0         // r8 = output array size (counter)

    // First pass: copy negative elements to output array
copy_loop:
    ldr r9, [r4], #4    // Load element from input array and increment pointer
    cmp r9, #0
    bge skip_element      // Skip if not negative
    str r9, [r6, r8, lsl #2]  // Store in output array
    add r8, r8, #1           // Increment output size
skip_element:
    subs r5, r5, #1
    bne copy_loop

    // Store the size of the output array
    str r8, [r7]

    // If output array is empty or has only one element, we're done
    cmp r8, #2
    blt done

    // Bubble sort the output array in descending order
    sub r5, r8, #1      // r5 = output size - 1 (for outer loop)

outer_loop:
    mov r9, #0        // r9 = swapped flag
    mov r10, #0        // r10 = inner loop counter

inner_loop:
    lsl r11, r10, #2
    add r11, r6, r11    // r11 = address of current element
    ldr r0, [r11]       // r0 = current element
```

```
    ldr r1, [r11, #4]    // r1 = next element
    cmp r0, r1
    bge no_swap          // If current >= next, no swap
                         // needed (changed from ble to bge)

    // Swap elements
    str r1, [r11]
    str r0, [r11, #4]
    mov r9, #1           // Set swapped flag

no_swap:
    add r10, r10, #1     // Increment inner loop counter
    cmp r10, r5
    blt inner_loop
    cmp r9, #0           // Check if any swaps occurred
    beq done             // If no swaps, array is sorted

    subs r5, r5, #1      // Decrement outer loop counter
    bne outer_loop

done:
    pop {r4-r11, pc}
```

Here are the key changes made to convert the function from ascending to descending order:

1. The function name has been changed from
    sort_negative_ascending to **sort_negative_descending**.
2. In the sorting phase, the comparison logic has been modified:

```
    cmp r0, r1
    bge no_swap          // If current >= next, no swap
                         // needed (changed from ble to bge)
```

This change means we only swap elements if the current element is less than the next element, resulting in a descending order sort for negative numbers (e.g., -1 > -3 > -5).

The C code that calls the **sort_negative_descending** function is shown in **Listing 59**.

Listing 59.

```c
#include <stdio.h>

extern void sort_negative_descending(int* iarr, int isize, int *oarr, int *osize);

int main() {
    int iarr[] = {25, 3, 38, -4, 2, -17, -8, 1, 44, -7};
    int isize = sizeof(iarr) / sizeof(iarr[0]);
    int oarr[10] = {0, 0, 0, 0, 0, 0, 0, 0, 0, 0};
    int osize = sizeof(oarr) / sizeof(oarr[0]);

    printf("Original array: ");
    for (int i = 0; i < isize; i++)
        printf("%d ", iarr[i]);
    sort_negative_descending(iarr, isize, oarr, &osize);
    // Print sorted array
    printf("\nUpdated array: ");
    for (int i = 0; i < osize; i++)
        printf("%d ", oarr[i]);
    printf("\n");
    return 0;
}
```

The application produces the following output:

Original array: 25 3 38 -4 2 -17 -8 1 44 -7
Updated array: -4 -7 -8 -17

Example 34

Here's (**Listing 60**) an ARM assembly function **sort_range_ascending** that sorts elements from an integer array falling in the range [-10, 10] in ascending order. This function will filter the elements within the specified range and then sort them.
Compared with previous examples, we've added range checking:

```
mov r12, #10      // r12 = range limit (10)
cmp r9, r12
```

```
bgt skip_element    // Skip if > 10
mvn r10, r12        // r10 = -11 (bitwise NOT of 10)
cmp r9, r10
ble skip_element    // Skip if <= -11
```

This checks if the element is in the range [-10, 10].

Listing 60.

```
.syntax unified
.arch armv7-a
.thumb
.global sort_range_ascending
.section .text
sort_range_ascending:
    push {r4-r12, lr}
    mov r4, r0      // r4 = input array address
    mov r5, r1      // r5 = input array size
    mov r6, r2      // r6 = output array address
    mov r7, r3      // r7 = address to store output size
    mov r8, #0      // r8 = output array size (counter)
    mov r12, #10    // r12 = range limit (10)

    // First pass: copy elements in range [-10, 10] to output array
copy_loop:
    ldr r9, [r4], #4    // Load element from input array and increment pointer
    cmp r9, r12
    bgt skip_element    // Skip if > 10
    mvn r10, r12        // r10 = -11 (bitwise NOT of 10)
    cmp r9, r10
    ble skip_element    // Skip if <= -11
    str r9, [r6, r8, lsl #2]  // Store in output array
    add r8, r8, #1          // Increment output size
skip_element:
    subs r5, r5, #1
    bne copy_loop

    // Store the size of the output array
    str r8, [r7]
```

```
// If output array is empty or has only one element, we're done
cmp r8, #2
blt done

// Bubble sort the output array in ascending order
sub r5, r8, #1      // r5 = output size - 1 (for outer loop)

outer_loop:
    mov r9, #0        // r9 = swapped flag
    mov r10, #0       // r10 = inner loop counter

inner_loop:
    lsl r11, r10, #2
    add r11, r6, r11  // r11 = address of current element
    ldr r0, [r11]     // r0 = current element
    ldr r1, [r11, #4] // r1 = next element

    cmp r0, r1
    ble no_swap       // If current <= next, no swap needed

    // Swap elements
    str r1, [r11]
    str r0, [r11, #4]
    mov r9, #1        // Set swapped flag

no_swap:
    add r10, r10, #1  // Increment inner loop counter
    cmp r10, r5
    blt inner_loop

    cmp r9, #0        // Check if any swaps occurred
    beq done          // If no swaps, array is sorted

    subs r5, r5, #1   // Decrement outer loop counter
    bne outer_loop

done:
    pop {r4-r12, pc}
```

In this function, the sorting logic remains the same as in the previous ascending order sort, as it's already set up to sort in ascending order. The resulting output array will contain all elements from the input array that fall in the range [-10, 10], sorted in ascending order.

The C code that calls the **sort_range_ascending** function looks like the following (**Listing 61**).

Listing 61.

```
#include <stdio.h>

extern void sort_range_ascending(int* iarr, int isize, int *oarr, int *osize);

int main() {
    int iarr[] = {25, 3, 38, -4, 2, -17, -8, 1, 44, -7};
    int isize = sizeof(iarr) / sizeof(iarr[0]);
    int oarr[10] = {0, 0, 0, 0, 0, 0, 0, 0, 0, 0};
    int osize = sizeof(oarr) / sizeof(oarr[0]);

    printf("Original array: ");
for (int i = 0; i < isize; i++)
    printf("%d ", iarr[i]);
sort_range_ascending(iarr, isize, oarr, &osize);
// Print sorted array
printf("\nUpdated array: ");
for (int i = 0; i < osize; i++)
    printf("%d ", oarr[i]);
printf("\n");
return 0;
}
```

The application produces the following output:

Original array: 25 3 38 -4 2 -17 -8 1 44 -7
Updated array: -8 -7 -4 1 2 3

Example 35

To change the ascending mode to descending one, we can modify the code of the function **sort_range_ascending**.

Here are the key changes made to convert the function from ascending to descending order:

- The function name has been changed from **sort_range_ascending** to **sort_range_descending**.
- In the sorting phase, the comparison logic has been modified:

```
cmp r0, r1
bge no_swap        // If current >= next, no swap
                   // needed (changed from ble to bge)
```

This change means we only swap elements if the current element is less than the next element, resulting in a descending order sort. The source code of the **sort_range_descending** function is shown in **Listing 62**.

Listing 62.

```
.syntax unified
.arch armv7-a
.thumb
.global sort_range_descending
.section .text
sort_range_descending:
    push {r4-r12, lr}
    mov r4, r0        // r4 = input array address
    mov r5, r1        // r5 = input array size
    mov r6, r2        // r6 = output array address
    mov r7, r3        // r7 = address to store output size
    mov r8, #0        // r8 = output array size (counter)
    mov r12, #10      // r12 = range limit (10)

    //First pass: copy elements in range [-10, 10] to output array
copy_loop:
    ldr r9, [r4], #4  // Load element from input array and increment pointer
    cmp r9, r12
    bgt skip_element  // Skip if > 10
    mvn r10, r12      // r10 = -11 (bitwise NOT of 10)
    cmp r9, r10
    ble skip_element  // Skip if <= -11
```

```
    str r9, [r6, r8, lsl #2]  // Store in output array
    add r8, r8, #1            // Increment output size
skip_element:
    subs r5, r5, #1
    bne copy_loop

    // Store the size of the output array
    str r8, [r7]

    // If output array is empty or has only one element, we're done
    cmp r8, #2
    blt done

    // Bubble sort the output array in descending order
    sub r5, r8, #1     // r5 = output size - 1 (for outer loop)

outer_loop:
    mov r9, #0        // r9 = swapped flag
    mov r10, #0       // r10 = inner loop counter

inner_loop:
    lsl r11, r10, #2
    add r11, r6, r11    // r11 = address of current element
    ldr r0, [r11]       // r0 = current element
    ldr r1, [r11, #4]   // r1 = next element

    cmp r0, r1
    bge no_swap        // If current >= next, no swap needed
                       // (changed from ble to bge)

    // Swap elements
    str r1, [r11]
    str r0, [r11, #4]
    mov r9, #1         // Set swapped flag

no_swap:
    add r10, r10, #1   // Increment inner loop counter
    cmp r10, r5
    blt inner_loop
```

```
cmp r9, #0      // Check if any swaps occurred
beq done        // If no swaps, array is sorted

subs r5, r5, #1    // Decrement outer loop counter
bne outer_loop
```

done:
```
pop {r4-r12, pc}
```

The resulting output array will contain all elements from the input array that fall in the range [-10, 10], now sorted in descending order (from highest to lowest).

As you correctly observed, this modification was indeed quite simple, involving only a change in the comparison logic. This demonstrates the flexibility of the bubble sort algorithm and how easily it can be adapted to different sorting requirements while maintaining the same filtering logic.

The C code that calls the **sort_range_descending** function is shown in **Listing 63**.

Listing 63.

```c
#include <stdio.h>

extern void sort_range_descending(int* iarr, int isize, int *oarr, int *osize);

int main() {
    int iarr[] = {25, 3, 38, -4, 2, -17, -8, 1, 44, -7};
    int isize = sizeof(iarr) / sizeof(iarr[0]);
    int oarr[10] = {0, 0, 0, 0, 0, 0, 0, 0, 0, 0};
    int osize = sizeof(oarr) / sizeof(oarr[0]);

    printf("Original array: ");
    for (int i = 0; i < isize; i++)
        printf("%d ", iarr[i]);
    sort_range_descending(iarr, isize, oarr, &osize);
    // Print sorted array
    printf("\nUpdated array: ");
    for (int i = 0; i < osize; i++)
        printf("%d ", oarr[i]);
```

```
printf("\n");
    return 0;
}
```

The application produces the following output:

Original array: 25 3 38 -4 2 -17 -8 1 44 -7
Updated array: 3 2 1 -4 -7 -8

Example 36

In this example, the assembly function **sum_array** (**Listing 64**) calculates the sum of the element of an integer array.

Listing 64.

```
.syntax unified
.arch armv7-a
.thumb
.global sum_array
.section .text
sum_array:
    cmp    r1, #0        // Compare size with 0
    beq    end_sum       // If size is 0, return 0
    mov    r2, #0        // r2 will hold the sum, initialize to 0

loop:
    ldr    r3, [r0], #4  // Load array element into r3, post-increment r0
    add    r2, r2, r3    // Add element to the sum in r2
    subs   r1, r1, #1    // Decrement size (r1)
    bne    loop          // If size != 0, continue loop

end_sum:
    mov    r0, r2        // Move the sum into r0 (return value)
    bx     lr            // Return from function
```

Explanation:
- The array address is passed in **r0**, and the size of the array in **r1**.

- The function initializes **r2** to 0 to store the sum.
- The loop iterates over the array, loading each element from memory into **r3** and adding it to **r2**.
- After processing each element, it decrements the size and loops until the size becomes 0.
- Finally, the sum is moved into **r0**, which is the return register in ARM, and the function returns using `bx lr`.

The C code that calls the function **sum_array** is shown in **Listing 65**.

Listing 65.

```
#include <stdio.h>

extern int sum_array(int* iarr, int isize);

int main() {
    int iarr[] = {25, 3, 8, -4, 2, -7, -8, 1, 4, -7};
    int isize = sizeof(iarr) / sizeof(iarr[0]);
    int sum = sum_array(iarr, isize);
    printf("Sum = %d\n", sum);
    return 0;
}
```

The application produces the following output:

Sum = 17

Example 37

Here's the ARM assembly function **sum_positive_elements** (**Listing 66**) that calculates the sum of positive elements in an integer array. The function will skip any negative or zero elements.

Listing 66.

```
.syntax unified
.arch armv7-a
```

```
.thumb
.global sum_positive_elements
.section .text
sum_positive_elements:
    cmp    r1, #0        // Compare size with 0
    beq    end_sum       // If size is 0, return 0
    mov    r2, #0        // r2 will hold the sum, initialize to 0

loop:
    ldr    r3, [r0], #4  // Load array element into r3, post-increment r0
    cmp    r3, #0        // Compare the element with 0
    ble    skip          // If element <= 0, skip adding it
    add    r2, r2, r3    // Add positive element to the sum in r2
skip:
    subs   r1, r1, #1    // Decrement size (r1)
    bne    loop          // If size != 0, continue loop
end_sum:
    mov    r0, r2        // Move the sum into r0 (return value)
    bx     lr            // Return from function
```

Changes from the Original Code of the function sum_array:

- After loading each element into **r3**, the element is compared with 0 using `cmp r3, #0`.
- If the element is less than or equal to 0 (`ble`), it jumps to the **skip** label without adding the value to the sum.
- Only positive elements are added to the sum in **r2**.

The C code that calls the function **sum_positive_elements** looks like the following (**Listing 67**).

Listing 67.

```
#include <stdio.h>

extern int sum_positive_elements(int* iarr, int isize);

int main() {
    int iarr[] = {25, 3, 8, -4, 2, -7, -8, 1, 4, -7};
    int isize = sizeof(iarr) / sizeof(iarr[0]);
    int sum = sum_positive_elements(iarr, isize);
```

```c
    printf("Sum of positives: %d\n", sum);
    return 0;
}
```

The application produces the following output:

Sum of positives: 43

Example 38

We can easily modify the function **sum_positive_elements** to calculate the sum of only negative elements. The key change is to check for negative values and sum them up, while skipping non-negative elements. Here's the modified version named **sum_negative_elements (Listing 68)**.

Listing 68.

```asm
.syntax unified
.arch armv7-a
.thumb
.global sum_negative_elements
.section .text
sum_negative_elements:
    cmp    r1, #0        // Compare size with 0
    beq    end_sum       // If size is 0, return 0
    mov    r2, #0        // r2 will hold the sum, initialize to 0

loop:
    ldr    r3, [r0], #4  // Load array element into r3, post-increment r0
    cmp    r3, #0        // Compare the element with 0
    bge    skip          // If element >= 0, skip adding it
    add    r2, r2, r3    // Add negative element to the sum in r2
skip:
    subs   r1, r1, #1    // Decrement size (r1)
    bne    loop          // If size != 0, continue loop
end_sum:
    mov    r0, r2        // Move the sum into r0 (return value)
    bx     lr            // Return from function
```

Explanation:
- The comparison instruction `cmp r3, #0` now uses `bge` (branch if greater than or equal) to skip non-negative elements.
- Only negative elements are added to the sum stored in **r2**.

The C code that calls the function **sum_negative_elements** is shown in **Listing 69**.

Listing 69.

```
#include <stdio.h>

extern int sum_negative_elements(int* iarr, int isize);

int main() {
    int iarr[] = {25, 3, 8, -4, 2, -7, -8, 1, 4, -7};
    int isize = sizeof(iarr) / sizeof(iarr[0]);
    int sum = sum_negative_elements(iarr, isize);
    printf("Sum of negatives: %d\n", sum);
    return 0;
}
```
The application produces the following output:

Sum of negatives: -26

Example 39

If we need to calculate the sum of elements within a specific range, such as [−10,10], we can adjust the function to include two comparisons: one to check if the element is greater than or equal to −10, and another to check if it is less than or equal to 10. Only elements that satisfy both conditions will be added to the sum.
Here's the ARM assembly code of the function **sum_in_range** (**Listing 70**) that implements this operation.

Listing 70.

.syntax unified

```
.arch armv7-a
.thumb
.global sum_in_range
.section .text
sum_in_range:
    cmp     r1, #0          // Compare size with 0
    beq     end_sum         // If size is 0, return 0
    mov     r2, #0          // r2 will hold the sum, initialize to 0

loop:
    ldr     r3, [r0], #4    // Load array element into r3, post-increment r0
    mov     r4, #-10        / Load -10 into r4 for comparison
    cmp     r3, r4          // Compare element with -10
    blt     skip            // If element < -10, skip this element
    mov     r4, #10         // Load 10 into r4 for comparison
    cmp     r3, r4          // Compare element with 10
    bgt     skip            // If element > 10, skip this element
    add     r2, r2, r3      // Add element within range to the sum in r2
skip:
    subs    r1, r1, #1      // Decrement size (r1)
    bne     loop            // If size != 0, continue loop
end_sum:
    mov     r0, r2          // Move the sum into r0 (return value)
    bx      lr              // Return from function
```

Explanation:
1. The function first checks whether the size is 0. If so, it returns 0.
2. The loop iterates over the elements, and for each element:
    *   It checks if the element is greater than or equal to -10 using
        `cmp r3, #-10` and **blt skip** (branch if less than -10).
    *   Then it checks if the element is less than or equal to 10 using
        `cmp r3, #10` and **bgt skip** (branch if greater than 10).
3. If the element is within the range $[-10,10]$, it is added to the sum
    stored in **r2**.
4. The loop continues until all elements are processed, after which the
    sum is returned in **r0**.

The C code that calls the function **sum_in_range** is shown in **Listing 71**.

Listing 71.

```c
#include <stdio.h>

extern int sum_in_range(int* iarr, int isize);

int main() {
    int iarr[] = {25, 3, 8, -4, 2, 77, -92, 1, 4, -5};
    int isize = sizeof(iarr) / sizeof(iarr[0]);
    int sum = sum_in_range(iarr, isize);
    printf("Sum in range [-10, 10]: %d\n", sum);
    return 0;
}
```

The application produces the following output:

Sum in range [-10, 10]: 9

Example 40

The assembly code from the previous example can be optimized using an IT (If-Then) block, which is available in the ARM Thumb-2 instruction set. The IT block allows conditional execution of a series of instructions based on a single condition code.
Here's (**Listing 72**) the optimized code of **sum_in_range** using the IT block to reduce branching and improve efficiency.

Listing 72.

```asm
.syntax unified
.arch armv7-a
.thumb
.global sum_in_range
.section .text
sum_in_range:
    cmp    r1, #0        // Compare size with 0
    beq    end_sum       // If size is 0, return 0
    mov    r2, #0        // r2 will hold the sum, initialize to 0

loop:
```

```
ldr    r3, [r0], #4    // Load array element into r3, post-increment r0
mov    r4, #-10        // Load -10 into r4
cmp    r3, r4          // Compare element with -10
ite    ge              // If element >= -10,
                       //execute next instructions conditionally
movge  r4, #10         // Load 10 into r4 (only if element >= -10)
blt    next            // If element < -10,
                       // skip the rest and go to next iteration

cmp    r3, r4          // Compare element with 10
it     le              // If element <= 10, execute the next instruction
addle  r2, r2, r3      // Add element to sum (only if element <= 10)
next:
subs   r1, r1, #1      // Decrement size (r1)
bne    loop            // If size != 0, continue loop
end_sum:
mov    r0, r2          // Move the sum into r0 (return value)
bx     lr              // Return from function
```

Explanation of the Key Corrections:

1. **ITE (If-Then-Else) Block:**
   - The ITE block (**ite ge**) is used to handle the condition where the element is compared with -10. If the element is greater than or equal to -10, it proceeds with loading 10 for the upper bound comparison (**movge**), otherwise, it skips to the `next` label if the element is less than -10.

2. **Nested Comparison for Upper Bound:**
   - If the element is within the lower bound ($>= -10$), it proceeds to check whether the element is less than or equal to 10 using `cmp` and `it le`.
   - The `addle` instruction will only add the element to the sum if it is less than or equal to 10.

3. **Branching Structure:**
   - If the element is less than -10, the program branches directly to `next` to avoid unnecessary checks.
   - The overall control flow is streamlined with fewer branches, leveraging the power of the IT block for conditional execution.

With this corrected approach, the code efficiently sums up only those elements within the range $[-10,10]$.

The C code that calls the **sum_in_range** function shown in **Listing 73**.

Listing 73.

```
#include <stdio.h>

extern int sum_in_range(int* iarr, int isize);

int main() {
    int iarr[] = {-2, 13, -8, -4, 2, 17, -9, 11, 4, -1};
    int isize = sizeof(iarr) / sizeof(iarr[0]);
    int sum = sum_in_range(iarr, isize);
    printf("Sum in range [-10, 10]: %d\n", sum);
    return 0;
}
```

The application produces the following output:

Sum in range [-10, 10]: -18

Example 41

Here's an ARM assembly function **write_bytes** (**Listing 74**) that retrieves 4 bytes from an unsigned integer and writes those bytes to an array. The function takes two parameters: the address of the integer in **r0** and the address of the memory location where the bytes will be written in **r1**.

Listing 74.

```
.syntax unified
.arch armv7-a
.thumb
.global write_bytes
.section .text
write_bytes:
    ldr    r2, [r0]        // Load the 4-byte integer from
                           // memory (pointed by r0)
```

```
// Extract and store the first byte (least significant byte)
uxtb   r3, r2        // Extract byte 0 from r2 into r3
strb   r3, [r1], #1  // Store byte 0 into the array and increment r1

// Extract and store the second byte
lsr    r2, r2, #8    // Shift r2 right by 8 bits to get the next byte in LSB
uxtb   r3, r2        // Extract byte 1 from r2 into r3
strb   r3, [r1], #1  // Store byte 1 into the array and increment r1

// Extract and store the third byte
lsr    r2, r2, #8    // Shift r2 right by another 8 bits
uxtb   r3, r2        // Extract byte 2 from r2 into r3
strb   r3, [r1], #1  // Store byte 2 into the array and increment r1

// Extract and store the fourth byte
lsr    r2, r2, #8    // Shift r2 right by another 8 bits
uxtb   r3, r2        // Extract byte 3 from r2 into r3
strb   r3, [r1]      // Store byte 3 into the array (no increment needed)
bx     lr            // Return from function
```

Explanation:

- **ldr r2, [r0]**: Loads the 4-byte unsigned integer from memory into **r2**.
- The function extracts each byte using `lsr` (logical shift right) and `uxtb` (unsigned extend byte) to isolate the least significant byte.
- Each extracted byte is stored into the memory location provided by **r1**, using `strb` (store byte).
- The address **r1** is incremented after storing each byte to write them in successive memory locations.

This function will write the 4 bytes of the integer in little-endian order (from least significant byte to most significant byte).

The C code that calls the function **write_bytes** looks like the following (**Listing 75**).

Listing 75.

#include <stdio.h>

// Declare the ARM assembly function

```
extern void write_bytes(unsigned int *integer_addr, unsigned char
*array_addr);

int main() {
    unsigned int number = 0x12345678; // Example unsigned integer
    unsigned char byte_array[4];      // Array to store the 4 bytes

    // Call the assembly function
    write_bytes(&number, byte_array);

    // Print the bytes stored in the array
    printf("Bytes in array: %02X %02X %02X %02X\n",
        byte_array[0], byte_array[1], byte_array[2], byte_array[3]);

    return 0;
}
```

The application produces the following output:

Bytes in array: 78 56 34 12

Example 42

This example illustrates how to rewrite the **write_bytes** function to store the bytes of the integer in reverse order. Below (**Listing 76**) is the code of the function named **write_bytes_rev** that implements this task.

Listing 76.

```
.syntax unified
.arch armv7-a
.thumb
.global write_bytes_rev
.section .text
write_bytes_rev:
    ldr    r2, [r0]        // Load the 4-byte integer from
                           // memory (pointed by r0)
```

```
// Store byte 3 (most significant byte)
lsr    r3, r2, #24      // Shift r2 right by 24 bits to get byte 3 (MSB)
strb   r3, [r1], #1     // Store byte 3 into the array

// Store byte 2
lsr    r3, r2, #16      // Shift r2 right by 16 bits to get byte 2
uxtb   r3, r3           // Extract byte 2 into r3
strb   r3, [r1], #1     // Store byte 2 into the array

// Store byte 1
lsr    r3, r2, #8       // Shift r2 right by 8 bits to get byte 1
uxtb   r3, r3           // Extract byte 1 into r3
strb   r3, [r1], #1     // Store byte 1 into the array

// Store byte 0 (least significant byte)
uxtb   r3, r2           // Extract byte 0 into r3
strb   r3, [r1]         // Store byte 0 into the array

bx     lr               // Return from function
```

Explanation:

- The function now retrieves each byte in reverse order, starting from byte 3 (most significant byte).
- The bytes are extracted by shifting the integer by the appropriate number of bits and using the `uxtb` instruction to mask out the unwanted upper bits after each shift.
- Each byte is then stored in the array at the next available position, incrementing r1 after each `strb`.

Order of Storing:

1. Byte 3: Extracted by shifting the integer right by 24 bits ($r2 >> 24$).
2. Byte 2: Extracted by shifting the integer right by 16 bits and masking ($r2 >> 16$).
3. Byte 1: Extracted by shifting the integer right by 8 bits and masking ($r2 >> 8$).
4. Byte 0: Directly extracted by masking ($r2$ & 0xFF).

This code effectively reverses the order of bytes when writing them to the array.

The C code that calls the **write_bytes_rev** function is shown in **Listing 77**.

Listing 77.

```
#include <stdio.h>

// Declare the ARM assembly function
extern void write_bytes_rev(unsigned int *integer_addr, unsigned char
*array_addr);

int main() {
    unsigned int number = 0x12345678; // Example unsigned integer
    unsigned char byte_array[4];      // Array to store the 4 bytes

    // Call the assembly function
    write_bytes_rev(&number, byte_array);

    // Print the bytes stored in the array
    printf("Bytes in array: %02X %02X %02X %02X\n",
        byte_array[0], byte_array[1], byte_array[2], byte_array[3]);

    return 0;
}
```

The application produces the following output:

Bytes in array: 12 34 56 78

Example 43

Here's an ARM assembly function **compare_arrays** (**Listing 78**) that compares two integer arrays of the same size.
Function Description:
  1. **Parameters:**
     • **r0**: Address of the first array.
     • **r1**: Address of the second array.
     • **r2**: Size of the arrays (number of elements).
  2. **Return:**

- 0 if both arrays are equal.
- -1 if they differ.

Listing 78.

```
.syntax unified
.arch armv7-a
.thumb
.global compare_arrays
.section .text
compare_arrays:
    cmp r2, #0          // Check if the size is zero
    beq arrays_equal    // If size is zero, arrays are equal

compare_loop:
    ldr r3, [r0], #4    // Load a value from the first
                        // array and post-increment r0
    ldr r4, [r1], #4    // Load a value from the second
                        // array and post-increment r1
    cmp r3, r4          // Compare the values
    bne arrays_differ   // If values are not equal, jump to arrays_differ
    subs r2, r2, #1     // Decrement the size (counter)
    bne compare_loop    // If more elements, continue the loop

arrays_equal:
    mov r0, #0          // Return 0 if arrays are equal
    bx lr               // Return from the function

arrays_differ:
    mov r0, #-1         // Return -1 if arrays differ
    bx lr               // Return from the function
```

Explanation:
- **Main Loop**: The function compares elements from the two arrays. It uses post-increment addressing to traverse the arrays and compares values element by element.
- **Exit Conditions**: If all elements are equal, the function returns 0. If any elements differ, it returns -1 immediately.
- **Zero-Length Arrays**: If the size is zero, the arrays are considered equal, and the function returns 0.

The C code that calls the **compare_arrays** function is shown in **Listing 79**.

Listing 79.

```
#include <stdio.h>

// Declare the assembly function
extern int compare_arrays(int* array1, int* array2, int size);

int main() {
    int array1[] = {1, 2, 3, 4, 5};
    int array2[] = {1, 2, 3, 4, 5};
    int array3[] = {1, 2, 3, 0, 5};

    int size = sizeof(array1) / sizeof(array1[0]);

    // Compare array1 and array2 (they should be equal)
    int result = compare_arrays(array1, array2, size);
    if (result == 0) {
        printf("array1 and array2 are equal.\n");
    } else {
        printf("array1 and array2 are different.\n");
    }

    // Compare array1 and array3 (they should be different)
    result = compare_arrays(array1, array3, size);
    if (result == 0) {
        printf("array1 and array3 are equal.\n");
    } else {
        printf("array1 and array3 are different.\n");
    }
    return 0;
}
```

The application produces the following output:

array1 and array2 are equal.
array1 and array3 are different.

Example 44

We can modify the ARM assembly function **compare_arrays** in order to return the index of the first unmatched element instead of -1 if the arrays differ. Here's the assembly function **compare_arrays_index (Listing 80)** that returns -1 if the arrays are equal and the index of the first mismatch if they are unequal (including 0 for the first element):

Function Description:
1. **Parameters**:
   - **r0**: Address of the first array.
   - **r1**: Address of the second array.
   - **r2**: Size of the arrays (number of elements).
2. **Return**:
   - -1 if both arrays are equal.
   - Index of the first unmatched element if the arrays differ.

Listing 80.

```
.syntax unified
.arch armv7-a
.thumb
.global compare_arrays_index
.section .text
compare_arrays_index:
    cmp r2, #0          // Check if the size is zero
    beq arrays_equal    // If size is zero, arrays are considered equal

    mov r3, #0          // Initialize index counter to 0

compare_loop:
    ldr r4, [r0], #4    // Load a value from the first
                        // array and post-increment r0
    ldr r5, [r1], #4    // Load a value from the second
                        // array and post-increment r1
    cmp r4, r5          // Compare the values
    bne arrays_differ   // If values are not equal, jump to arrays_differ
    add r3, r3, #1      // Increment the index
    subs r2, r2, #1     // Decrement the size (counter)
    bne compare_loop    // If more elements, continue the loop
```

```
arrays_equal:
    mov r0, #-1        // Return -1 if arrays are equal
    bx lr             // Return from the function

arrays_differ:
    mov r0, r3        // Return the index of the first mismatch
    bx lr             // Return from the function
```

The C code that calls **compare_arrays_index** is shown in **Listing 81**.

Listing 81.

```c
#include <stdio.h>

// Declare the assembly function
extern int compare_arrays_index(int* array1, int* array2, int size);

int main() {
    int array1[] = {1, 2, 3, 4, 5};
    int array2[] = {1, 2, 3, 4, 5};
    int array3[] = {1, 2, 3, 0, 5};

    int size = sizeof(array1) / sizeof(array1[0]);

    // Compare array1 and array2 (they should be equal)
    int result = compare_arrays_index(array1, array2, size);
    if (result == -1) {
        printf("array1 and array2 are equal.\n");
    } else {
        printf("array1 and array2 differs at index %d.\n", result);
    }

    // Compare array1 and array3 (they should be different)
    result = compare_arrays_index(array1, array3, size);
    if (result == -1) {
        printf("array1 and array3 are equal.\n");
    } else {
        printf("array1 and array3 differs at index %d.\n", result);
    }
```

```
  return 0;
}
```

The application produces the following output:

array1 and array2 are equal.
array1 and array2 differs at index 3.

Example 45

In this example, an ARM assembly function **count_mismatch (Listing 82)** compares two integer arrays and returns the number of unmatched elements. The function takes three parameters:
- **r0**: the address of the first array.
- **r1**: the address of the second array.
- **r2**: the size of the arrays.

It will return the number of unmatched elements between the two arrays.

Listing 82.

```
.syntax unified
.arch armv7-a
.thumb
.global count_mismatch
.section .text
count_mismatch:
    push {lr}           // Save return address
    mov r3, #0          // Initialize the mismatch counter to 0

compare_loop:
    cmp r2, #0          // Check if size (r2) is 0
    beq end_compare     // If size is 0, exit the loop

    ldr r4, [r0], #4    // Load an element from array 1 (r0)
                        // and post-increment pointer
    ldr r5, [r1], #4    // Load an element from array 2 (r1)
                        // and post-increment pointer
```

```
    cmp r4, r5            // Compare the two elements
    beq skip_increment    // If they are equal, skip
                          // incrementing mismatch counter
    add r3, r3, #1        // Increment the mismatch counter
skip_increment:
    sub r2, r2, #1        // Decrement the size counter
    b compare_loop        // Repeat the loop

end_compare:
    mov r0, r3            // Move the mismatch count to r0 for return
    pop {lr}             // Restore the return address
    bx lr                // Return from function
```

Explanation:

1. The function initializes a counter (**r3**) to zero.
2. It loops over the elements of both arrays, comparing each element.
3. If an element in one array does not match the corresponding element in the other, the mismatch counter is incremented.
4. The loop continues until all elements are processed.
5. Finally, the function returns the number of mismatches in **r0**.

The C code that calls the function **count_mismatch** is shown in **Listing 83**.

Listing 83.

```c
#include <stdio.h>

// Function declaration
extern int count_mismatch(int* array1, int* array2, int size);

int main() {
    int array1[] = {1, 2, -3, 4, -11, 17, 35};
    int array2[] = {1, 2, 0, 4, 90, 17, 36};
    int isize = sizeof(array1) / sizeof(array1[0]);

    int mismatches = count_mismatch(array1, array2, isize);
    printf("Number of mismatched elements: %d\n", mismatches);
    return 0;
}
```

The application produces the following output:

Number of mismatched elements: 3

Example 46

In this example, we will consider the function **write_mismatch** (**Listing 84**) that stores the indexes of mismatched elements in an integer array.
The function takes 4 parameters:
- **r0**: the address of the first array.
- **r1**: the address of the second array.
- **r2**: the size of the arrays.
- **r3**: the address of an array where the mismatched indexes will be stored.

Listing 84.

```
.syntax unified
.arch armv7-a
.thumb
.global write_mismatch
.section .text
write_mismatch:
    push {lr}          // Save return address
    mov r4, #0         // Initialize the mismatch counter (r4) to 0
    mov r5, r3         // Copy the address of the mismatch
                       // index array into r5

compare_loop:
    cmp r2, #0         // Check if size (r2) is 0
    beq end_compare    // If size is 0, exit the loop

    ldr r6, [r0], #4   // Load an element from array 1 (r0)
                       // and post-increment pointer
    ldr r7, [r1], #4   // Load an element from array 2 (r1) and
                       // post-increment pointer

    cmp r6, r7         // Compare the two elements
    beq skip_increment // If they are equal, skip storing the index
```

```
    str r4, [r5], #4      // Store the current index in the mismatch index
                          // array and post-increment the pointer
skip_increment:
    add r4, r4, #1        // Increment the index counter
    sub r2, r2, #1        // Decrement the size counter
    b compare_loop        // Repeat the loop
end_compare:
    mov r0, #0            // Move 0 to r0 for return
    pop {lr}              // Restore the return address
    bx lr                 // Return from function
```

Explanation of Code:
1. The index of each mismatch is stored in the array whose address is passed in **r3**.
2. The address of the mismatch index array is stored in **r5** for future use.
3. After each mismatch, the current index (**r4**) is stored in the mismatch array, and **r5** is incremented to point to the next position in the array.
4. At the end, the function returns 0 in **r0**.

The C code that calls **write_mismatch** looks like the following (**Listing 85**).

Listing 85.

```c
#include <stdio.h>

// Function declaration
extern void write_mismatch(int* array1, int* array2, int size, int* mismatch_indexes);

int main() {
    int array1[] = {1, -2, 13, 4, 90, -1, 14};
    int array2[] = {1, 2, 0, 4, 90, 1, 12};
    int size = sizeof(array1) / sizeof(array1[0]);
    // Allocate space for mismatch indexes
    int mismatch_indexes[7] = { -1, -1, -1, -1, -1, -1, -1 };

    write_mismatch(array1, array2, size, mismatch_indexes);
```

```c
    printf("Mismatched indexes: ");
    for (int i = 0; i < size; i++) {
        if (mismatch_indexes[i] >= 0) {  // Check for valid index
            printf("%d ", mismatch_indexes[i]);
        }
    }
    printf("\n");
    return 0;
}
```

The application produces the following output:

Mismatched indexes: 1 2 5 6

Example 47

This example illustrates how to use an ARM assembly function to count the number of matched elements in two integer arrays of the same size (with elements in the range [-10, 10]):

Function Prototype:
The function named **count_matches_range** takes three parameters:
- **r0**: address of the first array.
- **r1**: address of the second array.
- **r2**: size of the arrays.

The result, the count of matched elements, is returned in **r0**. The source code of this function is shown in **Listing 86**.

Listing 86.

```
.syntax unified
.arch armv7-a
.thumb
.global count_matches_range
.section .text
count_matches_range:
    push    {r4, r5, lr}      // Save registers and link register
```

```
    mov    r3, #0            // r3 will hold the match count
    mov    r4, #0            // r4 will be used as an index
loop:
    cmp    r4, r2            // Compare index with size
    beq    end               // If index == size, exit the loop
    ldr    r5, [r0, r4, LSL #2]  // Load element from the first array
    ldr    r6, [r1, r4, LSL #2]  // Load element from the second array
    cmp    r5, r6            // Compare the elements
    bne    next              // If not equal, go to next iteration

    cmp    r5, #10           // Check if element > 10
    bgt    next              // If greater, skip
    cmp    r5, #-10          // Check if element < -10
    blt    next              // If smaller, skip
    add    r3, r3, #1        // Increment match count
next:
    add    r4, r4, #1        // Increment index
    b      loop              // Repeat the loop
end:
    mov    r0, r3            // Move match count to r0
    pop    {r4, r5, lr}      // Restore registers and return
    bx     lr                // Return to caller
```

Explanation:

- The function uses a loop to compare elements of two arrays.
- It checks whether the elements are equal and within the range [-10, 10].
- If both conditions are satisfied, the match count is incremented.
- The loop continues until all elements in the arrays have been compared.
- The final match count is returned in **r0**.

Register Usage:

- **r0**: holds the address of the first array and later the result.
- **r1**: holds the address of the second array.
- **r2**: holds the size of the arrays.
- **r3**: stores the count of matched elements.
- **r4**: is used as the index for array traversal.
- **r5** and r6: hold elements from the two arrays for comparison.

This function ensures that only elements fitting within the range of [-10, 10] are considered for matches.

The C code that calls the function **count_matches_range** is shown in **Listing 87**.

Listing 87.

```
#include <stdio.h>

// Declare the external assembly function
extern int count_matches_range(int* array1, int* array2, int size);

int main() {
    int array1[] = {1, -5, 7, 9, -10, 81, 10};
    int array2[] = {1, -5, 8, 9, -10, 73, 10};
    int size = sizeof(array1) / sizeof(array1[0]);

    // Call the ARM assembly function
    int matches = count_matches_range(array1, array2, size);

    // Print the number of matched elements
    printf("Number of matched elements: %d\n", matches);

    return 0;
}
```

The application produces the following output:

Number of matched elements: 5

Example 48

Here is an ARM assembly function **compare_and_store_greater** (**Listing 88**) that compares two integer arrays of the same size and writes the greater of the two elements being compared into a third array.

Function Prototype:

The function takes four parameters:

- **r0**: address of the first array.
- **r1**: address of the second array.
- **r2**: address of the third array (where the greater elements will be written).
- **r3**: size of the arrays.

The function will compare elements from the first two arrays and store the greater one in the third array.

Listing 88.

```
.syntax unified
.arch armv7-a
.thumb
.global compare_and_store_greater
.section .text
compare_and_store_greater:
    push    {r4, r5, r6, lr}    // Save registers and link register
    mov     r4, #0              // r4 will be the loop index

loop:
    cmp     r4, r3              // Compare index with size
    beq     end                 // If index == size, exit loop

    ldr     r5, [r0, r4, LSL #2] // Load element from the first array
    ldr     r6, [r1, r4, LSL #2] // Load element from the second array
    cmp     r5, r6              // Compare the two elements
    it      lt
    movlt   r5, r6              // If r5 < r6, move r6 to r5
                                // (store the greater one)
    str     r5, [r2, r4, LSL #2] // Store the greater value in the third array
    add     r4, r4, #1          // Increment the index
    b       loop                // Repeat the loop
end:
    pop     {r4, r5, r6, lr}    // Restore registers and return
    bx      lr                  // Return to caller
```

Explanation:

1. Loop through the arrays: The function uses a loop that runs until all elements of the arrays are compared.
2. Compare elements: At each iteration, elements from the first and second arrays are loaded into **r5** and **r6**.
3. Store the greater value: The greater value between the two is stored in the third array.
4. Update index: The index is incremented, and the loop repeats until the end of the arrays is reached.

Register Usage:
- **r0**: holds the address of the first array.
- **r1**: holds the address of the second array.
- **r2**: holds the address of the third array (where the greater elements are stored).
- **r3**: holds the size of the arrays.
- **r4**: is used as the index for traversing the arrays.
- **r5, r6**: are used to store the elements from the first and second arrays during comparison.

The C code that calls **compare_and_store_greater** is shown in **Listing 89**.

Listing 89.

```
#include <stdio.h>

extern void compare_and_store_greater(int* array1, int* array2, int* result, int size);

int main() {
    int array1[] = {2, 5, -3, 10, 7};
    int array2[] = {3, 1, 0, 8, 6};
    int result[5];
    int size = sizeof(array1) / sizeof(array1[0]);

    compare_and_store_greater(array1, array2, result, size);

    // Output the result
    for (int i = 0; i < size; i++) {
        printf("result[%d] = %d\n", i, result[i]);
```

```
    }
    return 0;
}
```

The application produces the following output:

result[0] = 3
result[1] = 5
result[2] = 0
result[3] = 10
result[4] = 7

Example 49

If we want to write the lesser of the two elements being compared into a third array, we can modify the function **compare_and_store_greater** from the previous example.
Here we should change the conditional check to `it gt` (greater than), followed by `movgt r5, r6` - this effectively stores the lesser of the two elements. Here's why:

- **cmp r5, r6**: Compares **r5** and **r6**.
- **it gt**: Executes the following instruction if the condition `greater than` is true.
- **movgt r5, r6**: If **r5** > **r6**, moves **r6** to **r5**, meaning **r5** will hold the smaller value.

This can be used to write the smaller value into the result array instead of the greater one. The source code of a modified function named **compare_and_store_lesser** is shown in **Listing 90.**

Listing 90.

```
.syntax unified
.arch armv7-a
.thumb
.global compare_and_store_lesser
.section .text
compare_and_store_lesser:
```

```
push   {r4, r5, r6, lr}    // Save registers and link register
mov    r4, #0              // r4 will be the loop index

loop:
cmp    r4, r3             // Compare index with size
beq    end                // If index == size, exit loop

ldr    r5, [r0, r4, LSL #2] // Load element from the first array
ldr    r6, [r1, r4, LSL #2] // Load element from the second array
cmp    r5, r6             // Compare the two elements
it     gt                 // If r5 > r6
movgt  r5, r6             // Move r6 to r5 (store the lesser one)

str    r5, [r2, r4, LSL #2] // Store the lesser value in the third array
add    r4, r4, #1          // Increment the index
b      loop               // Repeat the loop

end:
pop    {r4, r5, r6, lr}    // Restore registers and return
bx     lr                 // Return to caller
```

Explanation:

- The logic stores the lesser of the two compared values into the third array. If **r5** > **r6**, then **r6** is written into **r5**, so the lesser of the two values is saved.
- The rest of the logic remains the same, except that now the result array will hold the minimum values from the two arrays at each position.

Thus, the function **compare_and_store_lesser** can be used when we need to store the smaller of two elements being compared.

The C code that calls the function **compare_and_store_lesser** is shown below (**Listing 91**).

Listing 91.

```
#include <stdio.h>

extern void compare_and_store_lesser(int* array1, int* array2, int* result, int size);
```

```c
int main() {
    int array1[] = {2, 5, -3, 10, 7};
    int array2[] = {3, 1, 0, 8, 6};
    int result[5];
    int size = sizeof(array1) / sizeof(array1[0]);

    compare_and_store_lesser(array1, array2, result, size);
    // Output the result
    for (int i = 0; i < size; i++) {
        printf("result[%d] = %d\n", i, result[i]);
    }
  return 0;
}
```

The application produces the following output:

result[0] = 2
result[1] = 1
result[2] = -3
result[3] = 8
result[4] = 6

Example 50

Here is an ARM assembly function **concat_arrays** (**Listing 92**) that concatenates two integer arrays. The function takes four parameters:

- **r0**: Address of the first array.
- **r1**: Size of the first array.
- **r2**: Address of the second array.
- **r3**: Size of the second array.

The result will be stored in the same memory location as the first array, with the second array appended after the first one.

Listing 92.

```
.syntax unified
.arch armv7-a
```

```
.thumb
.global concat_arrays
.section .text
concat_arrays:
    push {r4, r5, lr}        // Save registers on stack

    mov r4, r0               // r4 holds the starting address of the first array
    mov r5, r1               // r5 holds the size of the first array
    add r4, r4, r5, LSL #2   // r4 points to the location after
                             // the last element of the first array
    mov r5, r3               // r5 holds the size of the second array

copy_loop:
    cmp r5, #0               // Check if the second array has any more elements
    beq done                 // If no elements left, exit loop
    ldr r6, [r2], #4         // Load an element from the second array and
                             //increment the pointer
    str r6, [r4], #4         // Store the element in the concatenated
                             // array and increment the pointer

    subs r5, r5, #1          // Decrement the size counter of the second array
    bne copy_loop            // Repeat the loop if there are more elements
done:
    pop {r4, r5, lr}         // Restore saved registers
    bx lr                    // Return to the caller
```

Explanation:

1. **Address calculation:** The concatenation starts by calculating the memory location right after the last element of the first array.
2. **Copy loop:** Each element of the second array is loaded from memory (**ldr r6, [r2], #4**) and stored into the first array's location (**str r6, [r4], #4**). The loop continues until all elements of the second array are copied.
3. **Return:** Once all elements are concatenated, the function returns to the caller.

The C code that calls the function **concat_arrays** looks like the following (**Listing 93**).

Listing 93.

```c
#include <stdio.h>

// Function prototype for the assembly function
extern void concat_arrays(int *array1, int size1, int *array2, int size2);

int main() {
    // Define two integer arrays
    int array1[10] = {1, 2, 3, 4, 5};   // Array 1 with 5 elements
    int array2[5]  = {6, 7, 8, 9, 10};   // Array 2 with 5 elements

    // Get the sizes of the arrays
    int size1 = 5; // Number of elements in array1
    int size2 = 5; // Number of elements in array2

    // Call the ARM assembly function to concatenate array2 into array1
    concat_arrays(array1, size1, array2, size2);

    // Print the concatenated array
    printf("Concatenated Array: ");
    for (int i = 0; i < size1 + size2; i++) {
        printf("%d ", array1[i]);
    }
    printf("\n");
    return 0;
}
```

The application produces the following output:

Concatenated Array: 1 2 3 4 5 6 7 8 9 10

Bit operations

Using ARM assembly for bit operations is highly effective, especially when performance and efficiency are critical. Assembly language provides direct access to hardware capabilities, minimal overhead, and precise control over the execution, making it ideal for low-level and performance-sensitive applications.

Example 1

Below is an example of an ARM assembly function **count_set_bits** (**Listing 1**) that calculates the number of set bits (also known as the population count) in an integer and returns the result to C code.

Listing 1.

```
.syntax unified
.arch armv7-a
.thumb
.global count_set_bits
.section .text
count_set_bits:
    // Input: r0 = integer
    // Output: r0 = number of set bits

    mov    r1, #0          // Initialize counter in r1 to 0
count_loop:
    cmp    r0, #0          // Compare r0 with 0
    beq    done            // If r0 is 0, all bits processed, exit loop
    ands   r2, r0, #1      // Extract the least significant bit
    add    r1, r1, r2      // Add it to the counter (r1)
    lsr    r0, r0, #1      // Shift r0 right by 1 bit
    b      count_loop      // Repeat until r0 becomes 0
done:
    mov    r0, r1          // Move the count to r0 (return value)
    bx     lr              // Return to the caller
```

Explanation:

- The function takes an integer in **r0** and counts how many bits are set to 1 in its binary representation.
- It uses a loop that checks the least significant bit (using the `ands` instruction) and increments the counter in **r1** if the bit is set.
- The input integer is right-shifted by 1 on each iteration until it becomes 0.
- Finally, the result (number of set bits) is returned in **r0**.

The C code that calls the ARM assembly function **count_set_bits** is shown in **Listing 2**.

Listing 2.

```
#include <stdio.h>

// Declaration of the ARM assembly function
extern int count_set_bits(int num);

int main() {
    int num = 29;  // Example number (binary: 11101, 4 set bits)

    // Call the ARM assembly function
    int set_bits = count_set_bits(num);

    // Print the result
    printf("Number of set bits in %d: %d\n", num, set_bits);
    return 0;
}
```

The application produces the following output:

Number of set bits in 29: 4

Example 2

In this example, an ARM assembly function **count_zero_bits** (**Listing 3**) calculates the number of zero (`0`) bits in a 32-bit integer and returns the result to C code.

Listing 3.

```
.syntax unified
.arch armv7-a
.thumb
.global count_zero_bits
.section .text
count_zero_bits:
    mov    r1, #0
    cmp    r0, #0
    beq    done
    mvn    r0, r0
count_loop:
    cmp    r0, #0
    beq    done
    ands   r2, r0, #1
    add    r1, r1, r2
    lsr    r0, r0, #1
    b      count_loop
done:
    mov    r0, r1
    bx     lr
```

Function Overview:
- The function counts how many zero bits are present in the binary representation of an integer.
- It performs a bitwise NOT operation on the input value to convert zeros to ones (and vice versa) and then counts the number of ones, which corresponds to the number of zeros in the original input.

Code Breakdown:

- **mov r1, #0**: Initializes **r1** to zero. This register will store the count of zero bits.
- **cmp r0, #0**: Compares the value of **r0** (the input integer) with zero.
- **beq done**: If the input integer in **r0** is zero, the program branches to the done label, skipping the loop because all 32 bits are zero, and the count is already zero.

- **mvn r0, r0**: Performs a bitwise NOT on **r0** (complement of all bits). This changes all 0s in **r0** to 1s and vice versa. This transformation allows the function to count the number of 1s in the complemented value, which corresponds to the number of 0s in the original value.
- **cmp r0, #0**: Checks if the current value of **r0** is zero. If so, all bits have been processed, and it branches to the **done** label.
- **ands r2, r0, #1**: Performs a bitwise AND between the current value of **r0** and 1. This isolates the least significant bit (LSB) and stores the result in **r2**. If the LSB is 1, it means the corresponding bit in the original value was zero.
- **add r1, r1, r2**: Adds the result in **r2** to **r1**, effectively counting how many bits have been 1 in the complemented value, i.e., how many zero bits in the original number.
- **lsr r0, r0, #1**: Logical shift right by 1 bit. This shifts the next bit into the LSB position for the next iteration.
- **b count_loop**: Jumps back to **count_loop** to repeat the process until all bits are processed.
- **mov r0, r1**: Moves the count of zero bits (stored in **r1**) back into **r0**, which is the function's return value.
- **bx lr**: Branches back to the caller, returning the result in **r0**.

Summary of Logic:
- The function first performs a bitwise NOT on the input integer to convert zeros to ones.
- It then counts the number of 1s in this complemented value, which corresponds to the number of 0s in the original integer.
- It returns the count of zero bits.

The C code that calls **count_zero_bits** is shown in **Listing 4**.

Listing 4.

```
#include <stdio.h>

// Declaration of the ARM assembly function
extern int count_zero_bits(int num);

int main() {
    int num = -226072;
```

```
// Call the ARM assembly function
int zero_bits = count_zero_bits(num);

// Print the result
printf("Number of zero bits in %d: %d\n", num, zero_bits);
return 0;
}
```

The application produces the following output:

Number of zero bits in -226072: 11

Example 3

In this example, the ARM assembly function **set_bit** (**Listing 5**) allows to effectively set a specific bit in an unsigned integer.
The function takes two parameters:
- The address of a 32-bit unsigned integer (**r0**).
- The index of the bit to set (0-31) in **r1**.

Listing 5.

```
.syntax unified
.arch armv7-a
.thumb
.global set_bit
.section .text
set_bit:
    PUSH   {r4, lr}        // Save r4 and return address (link register)
    LDR    r2, [r0]        // Load the unsigned integer from
                           // the address in r0
    MOV    r3, #1          // Load 1 into r3
    LSL    r3, r1          // Left shift 1 by the bit
                           //number (r1) to set the specific bit
    ORR    r2, r2, r3      // Set the specified bit in the
                           //integer by ORing it with r2
    STR    r2, [r0]        // Store the modified integer
```

```
                    //back to the memory address

    POP    {r4, lr}      // Restore r4 and return address
    BX     lr            // Return from the function
```

Explanation:

1. **PUSH {r4, lr}**: Save the value of register **r4** and the return address **lr** on the stack.
2. **LDR r2, [r0]**: Load the unsigned integer from the address in **r0** into register **r2**.
3. **MOV r3, #1**: Load the constant 1 into register **r3** for bit manipulation.
4. **LSL r3, r1**: Left shift 1 by the number of positions given in **r1** (the bit number). This creates a mask where the desired bit is set.
5. **ORR r2, r2, r3**: Set the specific bit in the unsigned integer by performing a bitwise OR between the integer and the mask.
6. **STR r2, [r0]**: Store the modified value back at the memory address in **r0**.
7. **POP {r4, lr}**: Restore **r4** and the return address (**lr**).
8. **BX lr**: Return from the function.

The C code that calls the function **set_bit** is shown below (**Listing 6**).

Listing 6.

```c
#include <stdio.h>

// Declare the external assembly function
extern void set_bit(unsigned int *num, unsigned int bit);

int main() {
    unsigned int num = 0x0;   // Initialize an unsigned integer to 0
    unsigned int bit = 3;       // Specify the bit number to set (e.g., 3rd bit)

    printf("Before: 0x%X\n", num); // Print the value of
                                    //num before calling set_bit
    // Call the assembly function to set the 3rd bit
    set_bit(&num, bit);
    printf("After: 0x%X\n", num); // Print the value of
                                    // num after calling set_bit
```

```
    return 0;
}
```

The application produces the following output:

Before: 0x0
After: 0x8

Example 4

It is easily to modify the function **set_bit** to clear a specific bit. In this example, the assembly function **clear_bit** (**Listing 7**) allows to effectively clear a specific bit in an unsigned integer.
The procedure takes two parameters:
- The address of a 32-bit unsigned integer (**r0**).
- The index of the bit to set (0-31) in **r1**.

Listing 7.

```
.syntax unified
.arch armv7-a
.thumb
.global clear_bit
.section .text
clear_bit:
    PUSH   {r4, lr}      // Save r4 and return address (link register)
    LDR    r2, [r0]      // Load the unsigned integer
                         //from the address in r0
    MOV    r3, #1        // Load 1 into r3
    LSL    r3, r1        // Left shift 1 by the bit
                         // number (r1) to create the bit mask
    MVN    r3, r3        // Invert the mask (NOT operation) to prepare
                         //for clearing the bit
    AND    r2, r2, r3    // Clear the specified bit by ANDing with the
                         //inverted mask
    STR    r2, [r0]      // Store the modified integer
                         //back to the memory address
    POP    {r4, lr}      // Restore r4 and return address
```

```
BX    lr              // Return from the function
```

Explanation of Changes:
  1. **MVN r3, r3**: This instruction inverts the bit mask. For example, if the bit mask is 00001000 (bit 3), `MVN` will change it to 11110111.
  2. **AND r2, r2, r3**: This performs a bitwise AND operation between the integer and the inverted mask. This clears the specific bit while leaving the other bits unchanged.

The C code that calls the function **clear_bit** is shown in **Listing 8**.

Listing 8.

```c
#include <stdio.h>

// Declare the external assembly function
extern void clear_bit(unsigned int *num, unsigned int bit);

int main() {
    unsigned int num = 0x1D;   // Initialize an unsigned
                               // integer to 29 = 0x1D = 11101
    unsigned int bit = 0;      // Specify the bit number to clear (e.g., 0th bit)

    printf("Before: 0x%X\n", num);  // Print the value of
                                    // num before calling clear_bit

    // Call the assembly function to set the 3rd bit
    clear_bit(&num, bit);

    printf("After:  0x%X\n", num);  // Print the value of
                                    // num after calling clear_bit

    return 0;
}
```

The application produces the following output:

Before: 0x1D
After: 0x1C

Example 5

In this example, the assembly function **toggle_bit** (**Listing 9**) allows to effectively toggle a specific bit in an unsigned integer.
The procedure takes two parameters:
- The address of a 32-bit unsigned integer (**r0**).
- The index of the bit to set (0-31) in **r1**.

Listing 9.

```
.syntax unified
.arch armv7-a
.thumb
.global toggle_bit
.section .text
toggle_bit:
    PUSH   {r4, lr}      // Save r4 and return address (link register)
    LDR    r2, [r0]      // Load the unsigned integer
                         // from the address in r0
    MOV    r3, #1        // Load 1 into r3
    LSL    r3, r1        // Left shift 1 by the bit
                         //number (r1) to create the bit mask
    EOR    r2, r2, r3    // Toggle the specified bit
                         // by XORing it with the mask
    STR    r2, [r0]      // Store the modified integer
                         // back to the memory address

    POP    {r4, lr}      // Restore r4 and return address
    BX     lr            // Return from the function
```

Explanation:
- **EOR r2, r2, r3**: The `EOR` (XOR) instruction toggles the specific bit in the unsigned integer. If the bit is set (`1`), it becomes cleared (`0`); if it's cleared (`0`), it becomes set (`1`).

The C code that calls **toggle_bit** is shown in **Listing 10**.

Listing 10.

```c
#include <stdio.h>

// Declare the external assembly function
extern void toggle_bit(unsigned int *num, unsigned int bit);

int main() {
    unsigned int num = 0xF;   // Initialize an unsigned
                              // integer to 0xF (1111 in binary)
    unsigned int bit = 1;     // Specify the bit
                              //number to toggle (e.g., 1st bit)

    printf("Before toggling: 0x%X\n", num);  // Print the value of num
                                             // before calling toggle_bit

    // Call the assembly function to toggle the 1st bit
    toggle_bit(&num, bit);
    printf("Toggled <1>: 0x%X\n", num);  // Print the value of num after
                                         // calling toggle_bit
    toggle_bit(&num, bit);
    printf("Toggled <2>: 0x%X\n", num);  // Print the value of
                                         //num after calling toggle_bit

    return 0;
}
```

The application produces the following output:

Before toggling: 0xF
Toggled <1>: 0xD
Toggled <2>: 0xF

Example 6

Below is an example of an ARM assembly function **reverse_bits** (**Listing 11**) that reverses the order of bits in a 32-bit integer value. The function takes a single parameter in **r0** and returns the result in the same register.

Listing 11.

.syntax unified

```
.arch armv7-a
.thumb
.global reverse_bits
.section .text
reverse_bits:
    rbit r0, r0
    bx   lr
```

Explanation:

To reverse the bits of an integer in ARM assembly, you can use the `RBIT` instruction, which is specifically designed for this purpose.

The C code that calls the function **reverse_bits** is shown in **Listing 12**.

Listing 12.

```c
#include <stdio.h>

// Declare the ARM assembly function
extern int reverse_bits(int num);

int main() {
    int num = 29; // Example integer
    int reversed;

    // Call the ARM assembly function
    reversed = reverse_bits(num);

    // Print the original and reversed values
    printf("Original: 0x%08X\n", num);
    printf("Reversed: 0x%08X\n", reversed);
    return 0;
}
```

The application produces the following output:

Original: 0x0000001D
Reversed: 0xB8000000

Processing character strings

Processing character strings with ARM assembly language involves several steps, including loading the string into memory, iterating through each character, and performing desired operations such as copying, comparing, or modifying characters. This section includes several examples that demonstrates how to use the ARM assembler to process character strings.

Example 1

Here's the ARM assembly function **reverse_string** (**Listing 1**) that reverses the string in-place by swapping characters from the start and the end until the middle is reached.
The function should take two parameters:

- The address of the string (a pointer to the first character) in **r0**.
- The length of the string in **r1**.

Listing 1.

```
.syntax unified
.arch armv7-a
.thumb
.global reverse_string
.section .text
reverse_string:
        push {r4, r5, lr}      // Save registers and link register

        cmp r1, #0             // Check if the length is zero
        beq done               // If zero, nothing to reverse
        sub r1, r1, #1         // r1 = length - 1 (index of the last character)
        mov r4, r0             // r4 = start pointer
        add r5, r0, r1         // r5 = end pointer (r0 + length - 1)
reverse_loop:
        cmp r4, r5             // Check if the start pointer
                               //has crossed the end pointer
        bge done               // If true, we're done
```

128

```
        ldrb r2, [r4]        // Load byte from the start pointer
        ldrb r3, [r5]        // Load byte from the end pointer
        strb r3, [r4]        // Store the byte from the end at the start
        strb r2, [r5]        // Store the byte from the start at the end
        add r4, r4, #1       // Move start pointer forward
        sub r5, r5, #1       // Move end pointer backward
        b reverse_loop       // Repeat the process
done:
        pop {r4, r5, lr}     // Restore registers
        bx lr                // Return to the caller
```

Explanation:

1. **Input Parameters**:
   - **r0**: Pointer to the character string (the address of the first character).
   - **r1**: Length of the string.
2. **Process**:
   - First, the function checks if the length is zero and returns if there is nothing to reverse.
   - The last index of the string (length - 1) is calculated and stored in **r5**.
   - The string is reversed in-place by swapping characters at the start and end. The process continues until the start pointer (**r4**) meets or crosses the end pointer (**r5**).

The C code that calls the **reverse_string** function is shown in **Listing 2**.

Listing 2.

```c
#include <stdio.h>

// Declare the ARM assembly function
extern void reverse_string(char* str, int length);

int main() {
    // Define a string to reverse
    char str[] = "ARM Assembly";

    // Get the length of the string excluding the null terminator
```

```c
int length = sizeof(str) - 1;

// Print the original string
printf("Original string: %s\n", str);

// Call the assembly function to reverse the string
reverse_string(str, length);

// Print the reversed string
printf("Reversed string: %s\n", str);

return 0;
}
```

The application produces the following output:

Original string: ARM Assembly
Reversed string: ylbmessA MRA

Example 2

In this example, an ARM assembly function **to_uppercase** (**Listing 3**) changes all characters in a string to uppercase. The function takes two parameters: the address of the string (**r0**) and its length (**r1**).

Listing 3.

```
.syntax unified
.arch armv7-a
.thumb
.global to_uppercase
.section .text
to_uppercase:
        PUSH    {r4, lr}        // Save r4 and link register
        MOV     r2, #0          // Initialize index to 0

loop:
        LDRB    r3, [r0, r2]    // Load byte from string (r0 + index)
        CMP     r3, #0          // Check if null terminator (end of string)
```

```
    BEQ    end_loop        // If end of string, exit loop

    CMP    r3, #'a'        // Check if character is lowercase (>= 'a')
    BLT    next_char       // If less, skip to next character
    CMP    r3, #'z'        // Check if character is lowercase (<= 'z')
    BGT    next_char       // If greater, skip to next character

    SUB    r3, r3, #32     // Convert to uppercase by subtracting 32
    STRB   r3, [r0, r2]    // Store back the uppercase character

next_char:
    ADD    r2, r2, #1      // Increment index
    CMP    r2, r1          // Compare index with string length
    BLT    loop            // If not done, repeat loop
end_loop:
    POP    {r4, pc}        // Restore r4 and return
```

Explanation:

1. **Input parameters**:
   - **r0**: Address of the string.
   - **r1**: Length of the string.
2. **Function behavior**:
   - Loops through each character in the string.
   - Checks if the character is a lowercase letter (between `a` and `z`).
   - Converts it to uppercase by subtracting 32 from its ASCII value.

The C code that calls the function **to_uppercase** is shown in **Listing 4**.

Listing 4.

```c
#include <stdio.h>

// Declaration of the ARM assembly function
extern void to_uppercase(char *str, int length);

int main() {
    char str[] = "Hello, World!";
    int length = sizeof(str) - 1;  // Exclude the null terminator
```

```
// Call the assembly function to convert the string to uppercase
to_uppercase(str, length);

// Print the modified string
printf("Uppercase string: %s\n", str);
return 0;
}
```

The application produces the following output:

Uppercase string: HELLO, WORLD!

Example 3

Here's an ARM assembly function **replace_dots_with_spaces** (**Listing 5**) that replaces all dot (`.`) characters with spaces (` `) in a null-terminated string. The function takes the address of the string as a parameter in register **r0**.

Listing 5.

```
.syntax unified
.arch armv7-a
.thumb
.global replace_dots_with_spaces
.section .text
replace_dots_with_spaces:
    push    {r4, lr}        // Save r4 and link register
    mov     r1, #'.'        // Character to find (dot)
    mov     r2, #' '        // Character to replace with (space)

loop:
    ldrb    r3, [r0], #1    // Load a byte from the string, then increment r0
    cmp     r3, #0          // Check if we reached the null terminator
    beq     done            // If null terminator, we're done
    cmp     r3, r1          // Compare the character with '.'
    bne     loop            // If not a dot, continue the loop
    strb    r2, [r0, #-1]   // Replace the dot with a space
```

```
    b    loop            // Repeat the loop

done:
    pop  {r4, lr}         // Restore registers
    bx   lr              // Return from the function
```

Explanation:
1. The string address is passed in **r0**.
2. The function scans the string byte by byte. When it finds a dot (`.`), it replaces it with a space (` `).
3. The loop continues until it reaches the null terminator (\0).

The C code that calls the function **replace_dots_with_spaces** looks like the following (**Listing 6**).

Listing 6.

```c
#include <stdio.h>

// Declare the assembly function
extern void replace_dots_with_spaces(char *str);

int main() {
    char myString[] = "Hello.World.This.is.a.test.";

    printf("Before: %s\n", myString);

    // Call the ARM assembly function to replace dots with spaces
    replace_dots_with_spaces(myString);

    printf("After: %s\n", myString);
    return 0;
}
```

The application produces the following output:

Before: Hello.World.This.is.a.test.
After: Hello World This is a test

Example 4

Below (**Listing 7**) is an ARM assembly function **compare_strings** that compares two character strings and returns 0 if the strings are equal, otherwise returns 1.

Listing 7.

```
.syntax unified
.arch armv7-a
.thumb
.global compare_strings
.section .text
compare_strings:
    push   {r4, lr}       // Save r4 and link register
    mov    r2, #0          // Set default return value (equal)

compare_loop:
    ldrb   r3, [r0], #1    // Load byte from the first string and increment r0
    ldrb   r4, [r1], #1    // Load byte from the
                           // second string and increment r1
    cmp    r3, r4          // Compare the characters
    bne    strings_not_equal  // If characters are not equal, branch
    cmp    r3, #0          // Check if we reached the null terminator
    beq    strings_equal   // If both characters are null, strings are equal
    b      compare_loop    // Continue comparing next characters

strings_not_equal:
    mov    r2, #1          // Set return value to 1 (not equal)

strings_equal:
    pop    {r4, lr}        // Restore registers
    mov    r0, r2          // Move the result into r0 (return register)
    bx     lr              // Return to the caller
```

Explanation:
- Input: **r0** is the address of the first string, **r1** is the address of the second string.
- Output: **r0** is the result: 0 if the strings are equal, 1 if they are not.

134

- The function compares characters of both strings byte by byte. If a mismatch is found, it sets the return value to 1.
- If both strings are equal up to their null terminators, it returns 0.

The C caller for the **compare_strings** function is shown in **Listing 8.**

Listing 8.

```c
#include <stdio.h>

// Declare the assembly function
extern int compare_strings(const char *str1, const char *str2);

int main() {
    const char *string1 = "Hello";
    const char *string2 = "Hello";
    const char *string3 = "World";

    // Compare two equal strings
    int result = compare_strings(string1, string2);
    printf("Comparing '%s' and '%s': %s\n", string1, string2, result == 0 ?
"Equal" : "Not Equal");

    // Compare two different strings
    result = compare_strings(string1, string3);
    printf("Comparing '%s' and '%s': %s\n", string1, string3, result == 0 ?
"Equal" : "Not Equal");
    return 0;
}
```

The application produces the following output:

Comparing 'Hello' and 'Hello': Equal
Comparing 'Hello' and 'World': Not Equal

Example 5

Here's an ARM assembly function **count_char_in_string** (**Listing 9**) that counts the occurrences of a specific character in a null-terminated string. The function takes the address of the string in **r0** and the specific character to count in **r1**. It returns the count in **r0**.

Listing 9.

```
.syntax unified
.arch armv7-a
.thumb
.global count_char_in_string
.section .text
count_char_in_string:
    push    {r4, lr}        // Save r4 and link register
    mov     r2, #0          // Initialize count to 0

count_loop:
    ldrb    r3, [r0], #1    // Load byte from the string and increment r0
    cmp     r3, #0          // Check for null terminator
    beq     done            // If null terminator, end loop
    cmp     r3, r1          // Compare current character with target character
    bne     count_loop      // If not a match, continue the loop
    add     r2, r2, #1      // If match, increment count
    b       count_loop      // Continue the loop

done:
    mov     r0, r2          // Move the count to r0 (return register)
    pop     {r4, lr}        // Restore registers
    bx      lr              // Return to the caller
```

Explanation:
1. **Input**:
   - **r0** contains the address of the string.
   - **r1** contains the specific character to count.
2. **Output**:
   - The result, which is the count of occurrences of the specific character, is returned in **r0**.
3. The function loops through the string, checking each character. When it finds a match with the target character, it increments the count.

4. The loop terminates when the null terminator (\0) is encountered.

The C caller for the function **count_char_in_string** is shown in **Listing 10**.

Listing 10.

```
#include <stdio.h>

// Declare the assembly function
extern int count_char_in_string(const char *str, char ch);

int main() {
    const char *myString = "Hello, world!";
    char targetChar = 'o';

    // Count the occurrences of 'o' in the string
    int count = count_char_in_string(myString, targetChar);

    printf("The character '%c' occurs %d times in \"%s\".\n", targetChar,
count, myString);
    return 0;
}
```

The application produces the following output:

The character 'o' occurs 2 times in "Hello, world!".

Example 6

In this example, the ARM assembly function **find_substring (Listing11)**
searches for a substring in a character string. If the substring is found, the
procedure returns the index of the first element of the substring to the main
C procedure. If the substring is not found, the procedure returns -1.

Listing 11.

```
.syntax unified
.arch armv7-a
.thumb
```

```
.global find_substring
.section .text
find_substring:
    push   {r4-r7, lr}          // Save registers
    mov    r3, r0               // r3 = address of main string
    mov    r4, r1               // r4 = address of substring
    mov    r5, #0               // Initialize index counter

main_loop:
    ldrb   r0, [r3]             // Load byte from main string
    cmp    r0, #0               // Check for null terminator
    beq    not_found            // If end of string, return -1

    bl     match_substring      // Call to check if substring matches at
current position
    cmp    r0, #0               // Check the result
    beq    found                // If result is 0 (match), return the index

    add    r3, r3, #1           // Move to the next character in the main string
    add    r5, r5, #1           // Increment index
    b      main_loop            // Continue searching

not_found:
    mov    r0, #-1              // Return -1 if substring is not found
    pop    {r4-r7, lr}          // Restore registers
    bx     lr                   // Return to caller

found:
    mov    r0, r5               // Return the index of the substring start
    pop    {r4-r7, lr}          // Restore registers
    bx     lr                   // Return to caller

match_substring:
    push   {r4, lr}             // Save r4 and lr
    mov    r6, r3               // r6 = address in main string
    mov    r7, r4               // r7 = address of substring

match_loop:
    ldrb   r0, [r6], #1         // Load byte from main string
    ldrb   r1, [r7], #1         // Load byte from substring
```

```
cmp    r1, #0              // Check if we've reached
                          // the end of the substring
beq    match_success      // If end of substring, we found a match
cmp    r0, r1             // Compare main string character
                          // with substring character
bne    match_fail         // If they don't match, return to main loop

b      match_loop         // Continue matching characters

match_success:
  mov    r0, #0            // Return 0 for a match
  pop    {r4, lr}          // Restore registers
  bx     lr                // Return to main function

match_fail:
  mov    r0, #1            // Return 1 for no match
  pop    {r4, lr}          // Restore registers
  bx     lr                // Return to main function
```

Explanation:
1. **Input:**
   - **r0** is the address of the main string.
   - **r1** is the address of the substring.
2. **Output:**
   - **r0** contains the index of the first occurrence of the substring or -1 if not found.

The function works by scanning the main string character by character. For each character in the main string, it checks if the substring matches starting from that character. If it finds a match, it returns the index of that position; otherwise, it continues searching. If the substring is not found, it returns -1.

The C code that calls the function **find_substring** is shown in **Listing 12**.

Listing 12.

```
#include <stdio.h>

// Declare the assembly function
extern int find_substring(const char *str, const char *substr);
```

```c
int main() {
    const char *mainString = "Hello, world!";
    const char *substring = "world";

    // Search for the substring
    int index = find_substring(mainString, substring);

    if (index != -1) {
        printf("Substring '%s' found at index %d in \"%s\".\n", substring,
index, mainString);
    } else {
        printf("Substring '%s' not found in \"%s\".\n", substring, mainString);
    }
    return 0;
}
```

The application produces the following output:

Substring 'world' found at index 7 in "Hello, world!".

Example 7

In this example, an assembly function **count_matched_elements** (**Listing 13**) searches for the matched elements in two character strings of the same length. The assembly procedure returns the number of the matched elements or 0 if no matched elements found.

Listing 13.

```
.syntax unified
.arch armv7-a
.thumb
.global count_matched_elements
.section .text
count_matched_elements:
    push    {r4-r6, lr}      // Save registers
    mov     r2, #0           // Initialize match counter to 0
```

```
match_loop:
    ldrb    r3, [r0], #1        // Load a byte from the first string and increment
r0
    ldrb    r4, [r1], #1        // Load a byte from the second string and
increment r1
    cmp     r3, #0             // Check if we've reached the null terminator
    beq     end                // If null terminator, end loop

    cmp     r3, r4             // Compare characters from both strings
    bne     match_loop         // If not a match, continue the loop

    add     r2, r2, #1         // If match, increment match counter
    b       match_loop         // Continue comparing the next characters

end:
    cmp     r2, #0             // Check if any matches found
    beq     no_matches         // If no matches, return 0
    mov     r0, r2             // Return the match count in r0
    pop     {r4-r6, lr}        // Restore registers
    bx      lr                 // Return to caller

no_matches:
    mov     r0, #0             // Return 0 if no matches found
    pop     {r4-r6, lr}        // Restore registers
    bx      lr                 // Return to caller
```

Explanation:

1. **Input:**
    - **r0** contains the address of the first string.
    - **r1** contains the address of the second string.
2. **Output:**
    - **r0** contains the count of matched elements, or 0 if no matches
      were found.

The function compares the two strings byte by byte. If a match is found, the match counter (**r2**) is incremented. The loop continues until the null terminator is reached in either string.

The C code that calls the function **count_matched_elements** is shown in **Listing 14**.

Listing 14.

```c
#include <stdio.h>

// Declare the assembly function
extern int count_matched_elements(const char *str1, const char *str2);

int main() {
    const char *string1 = "Hello, world!";
    const char *string2 = "Hello, there!";

    // Search for the matched elements
    int matches = count_matched_elements(string1, string2);

    printf("Number of matched elements: %d\n", matches);
    return 0;
}
```

The application produces the following output:

Number of matched elements: 8

Example 8

Here's an ARM assembly function **concatenate_strings (Listing 15)** to concatenate two null-terminated strings. The function appends the second string to the end of the first string. The first string should have enough space to accommodate the concatenated result.

Listing 15.

```
.syntax unified
.arch armv7-a
.thumb
.global concatenate_strings
.section .text
concatenate_strings:
    push   {r4-r7, lr}       // Save registers
    mov    r4, r0            // r4 = address of the first string (destination)
```

```
        mov    r5, r1             // r5 = address of the second string (source)

find_end_of_first_string:
        ldrb   r6, [r4]           // Load byte from the first string
        cmp    r6, #0             // Check if end of the first string
        beq    append_second_string    // If end, go to
                                        //append the second string
        add    r4, r4, #1         // Move to the next character in the first string
        b      find_end_of_first_string

append_second_string:
        ldrb   r6, [r5]           // Load byte from the second string
        cmp    r6, #0             // Check if end of the second string
        beq    done               // If end, we're done
        strb   r6, [r4]           // Store byte to the end of the first string
        add    r4, r4, #1         // Move to the next position in the first string
        add    r5, r5, #1         // Move to the next byte in the second string
        b      append_second_string    // Continue appending

done:
        strb   r6, [r4]           // Null-terminate the concatenated string
        pop    {r4-r7, lr}        // Restore registers
        bx     lr                 // Return to caller
```

Explanation:

1. **Input:**
   - **r0** contains the address of the first string (destination).
   - **r1** contains the address of the second string (source).
2. **Output:**
   - The first string (**r0**) will contain the concatenated result.

The function first locates the end of the first string by traversing it until the null terminator is found. It then appends the second string character by character until its null terminator is reached. Finally, it adds a null terminator to the end of the concatenated string.

The C caller for the **concatenate_strings** function looks like the following (**Listing 16**).

Listing 16.

```c
#include <stdio.h>
#include <string.h>

// Declare the assembly function
extern void concatenate_strings(char *dest, const char *src);

int main() {
    char str1[100] = "Hello, ";   // Make sure str1 has
                                  // enough space for concatenation
    const char *str2 = "world!";

    // Concatenate str2 to str1
    concatenate_strings(str1, str2);

    printf("Concatenated string: %s\n", str1);
    return 0;
}
```

The application produces the following output:

Concatenated string: Hello, world!

Example 9

In this example, an ARM assembly function **count_words_with_symbol** (**Listing 17**) counts the number of words beginning with a specific symbol. The separator between words is assumed to be a space.
The function takes two parameters:
- **r0**: A pointer to the null-terminated string.
- **r1**: The symbol to check for at the beginning of words.

Listing 17.

```
.syntax unified
.arch armv7-a
.thumb
.global count_words_with_symbol
```

```
.type count_words_with_symbol, %function
.section .text
count_words_with_symbol:
    // r0: pointer to the string
    // r1: the symbol to check for
    push {r4-r7, lr}
    mov r4, r0        // r4 = current character pointer
    mov r5, r1        // r5 = symbol to check
    mov r6, #0        // r6 = word count
    mov r7, #1        // r7 = flag for start of word (1) or middle of word (0)

    // Check if the string is empty
    ldrb r2, [r4]
    cmp r2, #0
    beq exit

count_loop:
    ldrb r2, [r4]
    cmp r2, #0        // End of string?
    beq exit

    cmp r2, #32       // Is it a space?
    bne not_space

    // It's a space, set flag for start of word
    mov r7, #1
    b continue

not_space:
    cmp r7, #1        // Are we at the start of a word?
    bne continue

    // We're at the start of a word, check if it matches our symbol
    cmp r2, r5
    bne no_match

    // It matches, increment word count
    add r6, r6, #1

no_match:
```

```
    // We're no longer at the start of a word
    mov r7, #0

continue:
    // Move to the next character
    add r4, r4, #1
    b count_loop

exit:
    mov r0, r6        // Return the word count
    pop {r4-r7, pc}
```

Explanation:
1. It initializes a counter (**r6**) to keep track of the number of matching words.
2. The function iterates through the string, character by character:
   - It checks if the current position is at the start of a word (either the beginning of the string or after a space).
   - If it's at the start of a word, it checks if the next character matches the given symbol.
   - If there's a match, it increments the word count.
3. The function continues until it reaches the end of the string (null terminator).
4. Finally, it returns the total count of words beginning with the specified symbol.

The C caller for the function **count_words_with_symbol** looks like the following (**Listing 18**).

Listing 18.

```
#include <stdio.h>

// Declare the assembly function
extern int count_words_with_symbol(const char *str, char symbol);

int main() {
    const char *text = "apple peach banana persimmon apricot plum pear
berry almond";
    char symbol = 'p';
```

146

```
// Count words starting with the symbol 'a'
int word_count = count_words_with_symbol(text, symbol);

    printf("Number of words starting with '%c': %d\n", symbol,
word_count);
    return 0;
}
```

The application produces the following output:

Number of words starting with 'p': 4

Example 10

It is easily to modify the assembly function **count_words_with_symbol** to return the index of the first word beginning with a specific symbol instead of counting all such words. The modified assembly function named **find_first_word_index** is shown in **Listing 19**.

Listing 19.

```
.syntax unified
.arch armv7-a
.thumb
.global find_first_word_index
.type find_first_word_index, %function
.section .text
find_first_word_index:
    // r0: pointer to the string
    // r1: the symbol to check for
    push {r4-r7, lr}
    mov r4, r0      // r4 = current character pointer
    mov r5, r1      // r5 = symbol to check
    mov r6, #0      // r6 = current word index
    mov r7, #1      // r7 = flag for start of word (1) or middle of word (0)

    // Check if the string is empty
    ldrb r2, [r4]
```

147

```
        cmp r2, #0
        beq not_found

search_loop:
        ldrb r2, [r4]
        cmp r2, #0        // End of string?
        beq not_found

        cmp r2, #32       // Is it a space?
        bne not_space

        // It's a space, set flag for start of word
        mov r7, #1
        b continue

not_space:
        cmp r7, #1        // Are we at the start of a word?
        bne continue

        // We're at the start of a word
        add r6, r6, #1    // Increment word index

        // Check if it matches our symbol
        cmp r2, r5
        beq found

        // We're no longer at the start of a word
        mov r7, #0

continue:
        // Move to the next character
        add r4, r4, #1
        b search_loop

found:
        mov r0, r6        // Return the current word index
        pop {r4-r7, pc}

not_found:
        mov r0, #0        // Return 0 if not found (assuming 0 means not found)
```

```
pop {r4-r7, pc}
```

Explanation of Changes:

1. Changed **r6** to keep track of the current word index instead of a character index.
2. The function increments the word index (**r6**) every time it encounters the start of a new word.
3. The function returns as soon as it finds a word starting with the specified symbol.
4. If no matching word is found, the function returns 0 (assuming 0 means "not found" in this context; we can change this to -1 or any other value if needed).

Note that this function considers the first word as index 1, not 0. If you prefer 0-based indexing, you can easily modify it by initializing r6 to -1 instead of 0 and incrementing it before checking the symbol.

The C code that calls the function **find_first_word_index** is shown in **Listing 20**.

Listing 20.

```c
#include <stdio.h>

// Declare the assembly function
extern int find_first_word_index(const char *str, char symbol);

int main() {
    const char *text = "apple peach raspberry persimmon apricot plum
strawberry pear berry almond";
    char symbol = 'r';

    // Count words starting with the symbol 'a'
    int first_index = find_first_word_index(text, symbol);

    printf("Index of the first word starting with '%c': %d\n", symbol,
first_index);
    return 0;
}
```

The application produces the following output:

Index of the first word starting with 'r': 3

Generating random numbers

Generating random numbers is essential in various applications and systems, particularly in embedded systems and microcontroller programming. Here are some common reasons why random numbers are needed:

1. **Cryptography and Security**
   - **Key Generation**: Random numbers are critical for generating cryptographic keys used in encryption and decryption processes. Secure communications often rely on random keys to ensure data privacy.
   - **Nonces and Salts**: Random numbers are used to create nonces (numbers used only once) and salts (random data added to inputs of hash functions) to protect against replay attacks, dictionary attacks, and to ensure data integrity.
2. **Simulations and Modeling**
   - **Monte Carlo Simulations**: Random numbers are used in Monte Carlo methods to model complex systems, such as financial markets, physical systems, and other probabilistic models.
   - **Random Sampling**: In statistical analysis and simulations, random numbers allow for the selection of random samples from a larger data set, which is essential for unbiased results.
3. **Games and Entertainment**
   - **Random Events**: In gaming, random numbers are often used to generate unpredictable events, such as dice rolls, card shuffles, or the behavior of non-player characters (NPCs).
   - **Procedural Generation**: Random numbers can be used to create varied and dynamic environments, levels, or content in games, enhancing replayability.
4. **Testing and Debugging**
   - **Stress Testing**: Random inputs are used to test the robustness of systems and software by simulating a wide range of conditions and potential user inputs.
   - **Fuzz Testing**: In security testing, random inputs are used to discover potential vulnerabilities by generating unexpected or malformed data.
5. **Data Encryption**

- **Initialization Vectors (IVs)**: In encryption algorithms, random IVs are used to ensure that the same plaintext encrypts to different ciphertexts each time, improving security.
- **Random Padding**: Random numbers may be used to add padding to plaintext before encryption, preventing certain types of cryptographic attacks.

6. **Randomized Algorithms**
   - **Load Balancing**: Randomized algorithms help distribute tasks or requests evenly across resources, preventing overloads and optimizing performance.
   - **Randomized Search and Sorting**: Certain algorithms use randomness to improve average-case performance or avoid worst-case scenarios, such as in quicksort.

7. **Machine Learning**
   - **Initialization of Weights**: In neural networks, random numbers are often used to initialize weights to prevent symmetry and ensure proper training.
   - **Data Shuffling**: Randomization is used to shuffle data before training models, ensuring that the model generalizes well and doesn't overfit.

8. **Randomized Decision-Making**
   - **Load Distribution**: Random numbers can help in distributing loads or making decisions where fairness or unpredictability is needed, such as in network routing.
   - **Randomized Algorithms**: In scenarios like randomized quicksort, randomness helps avoid worst-case performance.

9. **User Experience**
   - **Dynamic Content**: Random numbers can be used to create dynamic and personalized user experiences, such as randomly selecting content or recommendations.
   - **Animations and Effects**: In embedded devices with user interfaces, random numbers can introduce subtle variations in animations or effects, making the interface more engaging.

10. Sensor Data Simulation
    - Test Environments: Random numbers can simulate sensor data when actual sensors are not available, enabling testing of algorithms and systems under development.

Random numbers are foundational in these and many other areas, making them a critical aspect of system design and implementation in embedded systems and beyond.

There are various algorithms to generate pseudo-random numbers, each with different characteristics and complexity. Below are some common approaches to generating random numbers in assembly for Cortex-M microcontrollers:

Example 1

In this example, we use the **Linear Congruential Generator (LCG)** that is one of the simplest and oldest random number generators. It generates a sequence of numbers based on the following recurrence relation:

$$X_{n+1} = (a \times X_n + c) \bmod m$$

Where:

- X_n is the current state,
- **a, c**, and **m** are constants that define the generator.

The assembly function **lcg_random (Listing 1)** implements the LCG algorithm.

Listing 1.

```
.syntax unified
.cpu cortex-m4
.thumb
.global lcg_random
.type lcg_random, %function
.section .text
lcg_random:
    // Inputs: Current seed in r0
    // Output: Next random number in r0

    // Constants (a, c, m)
    LDR r1, =1664525       // a = 1664525
    LDR r2, =1013904223    // c = 1013904223
```

// m = 2^32 is implicit since result will wrap around in 32-bit register

// Step 1: Multiply the seed by a
MUL r0, r0, r1   // r0 = a * seed

// Step 2: Add c
ADD r0, r0, r2   // r0 = a * seed + c

// Step 3: Modulo m is implicit because of 32-bit overflow

// Return next random number in r0
BX lr   // Return to the caller

The C code that calls the assembly function **lcg_random** is shown in **Listing 2**.

Listing 2.

```
#include <stdio.h>

// Declare the assembly function
extern unsigned int lcg_random(unsigned int seed);

int main() {
    unsigned int seed = 12345;  // Initial seed value

    // Generate 10 random numbers using the LCG
    for (int i = 0; i < 10; i++) {
        seed = lcg_random(seed);  // Call assembly function to get the next
                                  // random number
        printf("RND number <%d>: %u\n", i + 1, seed);  // Print the
                                  //generated number
    }
    return 0;
}
```

Explanation:

1. **Assembly Function (lcg_random):**
   - The function takes an initial seed (**r0**) as input.

154

- It performs the LCG computation: $X_{n+1} = (a \times X_n + c) \bmod m$.
- The result is implicitly modulo m because of 32-bit overflow in the register.
- The new random number is returned in **r0**.

2. **C Code**:
   - The **lcg_random** function is declared as **extern** so it can be called from C.
   - The C program uses a loop to generate and print 10 pseudo-random numbers.
   - The seed is updated after each call, ensuring the sequence progresses.

3. **Result**: The generated random numbers are printed in sequence, based on the initial seed. Each new number is derived from the previous one using the LCG formula.

This approach will work on Cortex-M devices that support Thumb-2 instructions, such as the Cortex-M4 or Cortex-M7.

The application produces the following output:

RND number <1>: 87628868
RND number <2>: 71072467
RND number <3>: 2332836374
RND number <4>: 2726892157
RND number <5>: 3908547000
RND number <6>: 483019191
RND number <7>: 2129828778
RND number <8>: 2355140353
RND number <9>: 2560230508
RND number <10>: 3364893915

Example 2

In this example, we use the **XORShift** algorithm that is another lightweight pseudo-random number generator. It uses bitwise XOR and shift operations, making it very efficient for low-power devices like Cortex-M microcontrollers.
The basic algorithm is:

$$X_n \oplus = X_n << a$$
$$X_n \oplus = X_n >> b$$
$$X_n \oplus = X_n << c$$

where **a**, **b**, and **c** are shift values.

Below (**Listing 3**) is the assembly function **rnd_xorshift** that generates the pseudo-random numbers.

Listing 3.

```
.syntax unified
.cpu cortex-m4
.thumb
.global rnd_xorshift
.type rnd_xorshift, %function
.section .text
rnd_xorshift:
    // Input: Seed in r0
    // Output: Random number in r0

    // Step 1: Shift left and XOR
    MOV r1, r0        // r1 = X_n
    LSL r1, r1, #13   // r1 = X_n << 13 (=a)
    EOR r0, r0, r1    // X_n ^= (X_n << 13)

    // Step 2: Shift right and XOR
    MOV r1, r0        // r1 = X_n
    LSR r1, r1, #17   // r1 = X_n >> 17 (=b)
    EOR r0, r0, r1    // X_n ^= (X_n >> 17)

    // Step 3: Shift left and XOR
    MOV r1, r0        // r1 = X_n
    LSL r1, r1, #5    // r1 = X_n << 5 (=c)
    EOR r0, r0, r1    // X_n ^= (X_n << 5)

    BX lr             // Return X_n
```

The C code that calls **rnd_xorshift** looks like the following (**Listing 4**).

Listing 4.

```c
#include <stdio.h>
extern int rnd_xorshift(int seed);
int seed = 234;

int main(void) {
  for (int i = 0; i < 10; i++) {
    seed = rnd_xorshift(seed);
    printf("RND <%d> : %d\n", i+1, seed);
  }
  return 0;
}
```

The application produces the following output:

RND <1> : 62217316
RND <2> : -1358395528
RND <3> : 1125960171
RND <4> : -1642505317
RND <5> : 405161198
RND <6> : -943293741
RND <7> : 455068989
RND <8> : -1245999039
RND <9> : 835297432
RND <10> : -1097929515

Example 3

We can use the **Logistic map** simulation to generate pseudo-random numbers. The logistic map chaotic system is commonly expressed by the recursive relation:

$$x_{n+1} = r \times x_n \times \cdot (1 - x_n)$$

where **r** is a control parameter (typically between 3.57 and 4.0 to induce chaotic behavior), and x_n is the current value in the sequence (usually in the range [0, 1]).

To implement this in Cortex-A53 assembly, we will use floating-point arithmetic to compute the iterative function. The generated values can be interpreted as pseudo-random numbers. Below (**Listing 5**) is the assembly function **rnd_gen** written for Cortex-A53.

Listing 5.

```
.syntax unified
.cpu cortex-a53
.global rnd_gen
.type rnd_gen, %function
.section .text
rnd_gen:
    // Load two double-precision values into registers
    vldr.f64 d0, [r0]    // Load `r` from memory pointed by r0
    vldr.f64 d1, [r1]    // Load `x` from memory pointed by r1
    vmov.f64 d2, #1.0

    // Perform addition
    vsub.f64 d3, d2, d1   // d3 = d2 - d1 -> 1-x
    vmul.f64 d3, d3, d0   // d3 = d3 * d0 -> r*(1-x)
    vmul.f64 d3, d3, d1   // d3 = d3 * d1 -> x*r*(1-x)
    vmov.f64 d0, d3
    // Result is now in d0, which is
    // where C expects it for a double return value
    bx lr                 // Return to caller
```

Code Explanation:
1. **Loading Values**:
   - **vldr.f64 d0, [r0]**: Load the value of `r` (control parameter) from memory into register **d0**.
   - **vldr.f64 d1, [r1]**: Load the value of `x` (current value in the sequence) from memory into register **d1**.
   - **vmov.f64 d2, #1.0**: Load the constant value 1.0 into register **d2**.
2. **Performing the Logistic Map Calculation**:
   - **vsub.f64 d3, d2, d1**: Compute `1 - x` and store the result in **d3**. This step is equivalent to the term $(1 - x_n)$ in the logistic map formula.

158

- **vmul.f64 d3, d3, d0**: Multiply r (stored in **d0**) by the result of (**1 - x**) to get `r * (1 - x)` and store it in **d3**. This is part of the logistic map equation: `r * (1 - xn)`.
- **vmul.f64 d3, d3, d1**: Multiply the result by `x` to compute `x * r * (1 - x)` and store it in **d3**. This is the full logistic map equation: `$x_{n+1} = r * x_n * (1 - x_n)$`.

3. **Storing the Result:**
   - **vmov.f64 d0, d3**: Move the result of the logistic map equation into **d0**, which is the register where C expects the return value of a double-precision floating-point function.

4. Returning:
   - **bx lr**: Return from the function, with the result of the calculation stored in **d0**.

The C code that calls the assembly function **rnd_gen** looks like the following (**Listing 6**).

Listing 6.

```
#include <stdio.h>

extern double rnd_gen(double *r, double *x);

int main() {
    double r = 3.7; // Growth rate parameter
    double x = 0.5; // Initial population

    int iterations = 10; // Number of iterations
    for (int i = 0; i < iterations; i++) {
        x= rnd_gen(&r, &x);
        printf("<%d>: %f\n", i, x);
    }
    return 0;
}
```

The application produces the following output:

<0>: 0.925000
<1>: 0.256687
<2>: 0.705956

159

<3>: 0.768053
<4>: 0.659146
<5>: 0.831289
<6>: 0.518916
<7>: 0.923676
<8>: 0.260845
<9>: 0.713378

Example 4

There are several other chaotic systems that can be simulated to generate pseudo-random numbers. In this example, we will use the **Henon map**. This system is also used in various applications for generating pseudo-random numbers due to its sensitivity to initial conditions and unpredictability.
The **Henon map** is a discrete-time dynamical system described by the equations:

$$x_{n+1} = 1 - a \times x_n{}^2 + y_n$$
$$y_{n+1} = b \times \cdot x_n$$

Parameters `a` and `b` are constants. This system generates chaotic behavior when `a` and `b` are within certain ranges.
For the **Henon map**, optimal parameters to obtain chaotic behavior and pseudo-random number generation are:

a=1.4
b=0.3
These parameter values are commonly used because they result in chaotic dynamics, which are essential for generating pseudo-random numbers. With these parameters, the Henon map exhibits a sensitive dependence on initial conditions, leading to an unpredictable sequence of values, which can be interpreted as pseudo-random numbers.

Explanation of Parameters:
- **a**: This parameter controls the nonlinearity of the system. When a=1.4, the system displays chaotic behavior, producing a sequence of values that seems random.
- **b**: This parameter controls the stretching and folding of the phase space. At b=0.3, the system complements the chaotic behavior induced by a.

These values are optimal because they create the desired balance between order and chaos, producing a sequence of values that are highly sensitive to initial conditions, making them useful for pseudo-random number generation.

Important Notes:

- **Initial Conditions**: The initial values of x_0 and y_0 should typically be chosen randomly (but within the bounds of the system, such as between -1.5 and 1.5), as the Henon map's output is highly sensitive to initial conditions. This sensitivity helps create a more chaotic and pseudo-random sequence.
- **Chaotic Region**: For `a` and `b` outside of this range, the system may enter periodic or stable behavior, reducing its usefulness for random number generation.

Example:

We can start with the following values:

$x_0 = 0.1$
$y_0 = 0.1$

These initial values, along with **a**=1.4 and **b**=0.3, should generate a sequence of pseudo-random numbers suitable for your application.

Below (**Listing 7**) is the assembly function **rnd_genhm** for Cortex-A53 that generates pseudo-random numbers using the Henon map algorithm.

Listing 7.

```
.syntax unified
.cpu cortex-a53
.global rnd_genhm
.type rnd_genhm, %function
.section .data
  a: .double 1.4
  b: .double 0.3
  c: .double 1.0

.section .text
```

```
rnd_genhm:
  vldr.f64 d2, [r0]    // =x
  vldr.f64 d3, [r1]    // =y
  ldr r2, =a
  vldr.f64 d0, [r2]    // d0 = a = 1.4
  ldr r3, =b
  vldr.f64 d1, [r3]    // d1 = b = 0.3
  ldr r2, =c
  vldr.f64 d5, [r2]    // d5 = c

  vmul.f64 d4, d2, d2  // d4 = x_n^2
  vneg.f64 d4, d4      // d4 = -x_n^2
  vmul.f64 d4, d4, d0  // d4 = -a * x_n^2
  vadd.f64 d4, d4, d3  // d4 = -a * x_n^2 + y_n
  vadd.f64 d4, d5, d4  // d4 = 1 - a * x_n^2 + y_n -> x_(n+1)

  vmul.f64 d3, d2, d1  // d3 = b * x_n -> y_(n+1)
  vmov.f64 d2, d4      // Store x_(n+1) in d2
  vstr.f64 d3, [r1]
  vstr.f64 d2, [r0]
  bx lr
```

The C code that calls function **rnd_genhm** looks like the following (**Listing 8**).

Listing 8.

```
#include <stdio.h>

extern void rnd_genhm(double *x, double *y);
double x = 0.1;
double y = 0.3;

int main(void) {
for (int i1 = 0; i1 < 10; i1++)
{
rnd_genhm(&x, &y);
printf("<%f>\n", x);
}
  return 0;
```

162

}

The application produces the following output:

```
pi@raspberrypi:~/Apps/rnd_genhm/Debug $ ./rnd_genhm
<1.286000>
<-1.285314>
<-0.927046>
<-0.588775>
<0.236567>
<0.745018>
<0.293898>
<1.102579>
<-0.613782>
<0.803354>
<-0.087663>
<1.230247>
<-1.145211>
<-0.467038>
<0.351063>
<0.687346>
<0.443897>
<0.930341>
<-0.078580>
<1.270458>
```

Example 5

The **Middle Square** Method is another simple generator of pseudo-random numbers, though less commonly used due to its statistical weaknesses in some cases. We square the current number and take the middle digits as the next random number.
Algorithm:
- Square the current state.
- Extract the middle part of the result as the next state.

This method can have shorter periods than other algorithms and is sensitive to the choice of the initial seed.

Below (**Listing 9**) is the assembly function that implements this approach.

Listing 9.

```
.syntax unified
.cpu cortex-m4
.thumb
.global rnd_msq
.type rnd_msq, %function
.section .text
rnd_msq:
    // Input: Seed in r0
    // Output: Random number in r0

    // Step 1: Square the number
    MUL R0, R0, R0          // R0 = Xn^2

    // Step 2: Extract middle 16 bits (assuming 32-bit numbers)

    LSR R0, R0, #8          // Shift right to remove lower bits
    LDR R1, =0xFFFF0000
    BIC R0, R1              // Mask out the upper 16 bits
    BX LR                   // Return middle square result
```

The application produces the following output:

RND <1> : 448
RND <2> : 784
RND <3> : 2401
RND <4> : 22518
RND <5> : 14624
RND <6> : 48964
RND <7> : 59018
RND <8> : 40002
RND <9> : 24705
RND <10> : 24833

Processing single-precision floating-point numbers

In this section, we consider the single-precision floating-point operations. All assembly procedures in this section were developed using a Cortex-M4F processor, therefore we should follow the C calling conventions described below.

The C calling conventions for ARM procedures operating with single-precision floating-point numbers, specifically for Cortex-M4F, are defined by the ARM Architecture Procedure Call Standard (AAPCS). Here are the key points:

1. **Parameter Passing**:
   - The first 4 single-precision float arguments are passed in registers **S0** to **S3**.
   - Any additional float arguments are passed on the stack.

2. **Return Value**: Single-precision float return values are placed in S0.

3. **Register Usage**:
   - **S0-S15** are considered scratch registers and do not need to be preserved across function calls.
   - **S16-S31** are callee-saved registers. If used, they must be preserved by the called function.

4. **Stack Alignment**: The stack must be 8-byte aligned at the point of function call.

5. **Function Prologue/Epilogue**:
   - If **S16-S31** are used, they should be saved at the beginning of the function (prologue) and restored before returning (epilogue).

6. **Variadic Functions**:
   - For variadic functions (like printf), floating-point arguments are passed in general-purpose registers (**r0-r3**) or on the stack, not in S registers.

165

7. **Mixed Integer and Float Arguments:**
   - When a function has both integer and float arguments, the allocation of arguments to registers is done as if all arguments were integers or integer-sized.

8. **FPSCR (Floating-Point Status and Control Register):**
   - The **FPSCR** is not preserved across function calls. If a function changes **FPSCR** flags or modes, it's responsible for saving and restoring the original value if needed.

9. **Thumb State:**
   - Cortex-M4F always operates in Thumb state, so all function calls and returns use Thumb instructions.

These conventions allow for efficient parameter passing and return of floating-point values, taking advantage of the Cortex-M4F's floating-point unit. They also ensure compatibility between different compiled C functions and libraries.

Remember that while these are the standard conventions, some compilers might offer options to modify these behaviors for optimization purposes. Always refer to your specific compiler's documentation for any potential deviations from the standard.

Example 1

In this example, the assembly function **add2fp (Listing 1)** calculates the sum of two single-precision numbers and returns the result to the C procedure.

Listing 1.

```
.syntax unified
.cpu cortex-m4
.thumb
.type add2fp, %function
.global add2fp
.section .text
add2fp:
  vadd.f32 s0, s1
  bx lr
```

This function uses ARM calling convention: For ARM processors with a floating-point unit (which includes Cortex-M4F), the ARM Architecture Procedure Call Standard (AAPCS) specifies that the first few floating-point arguments are passed in **S0**, **S1**, **S2**, etc. Let's break down the code:

1. **Input parameters**: The first float is already in **S0**, and the second float is in **S1** when the function is called.
2. **Return value**: The AAPCS also specifies that floating-point return values should be in **S0**. By performing the addition with **S0** as the destination, we're automatically placing the result where it needs to be for the return value.
3. The instruction `vadd.f32 s0, s1` performs addition **S0** = **S0** + **S1**.

The C code that calls the function **add2fp** looks like the following (**Listing 2**).

Listing 2.

```
#include <stdio.h>

extern float add2fp(float f1, float f2);

float f1 = -0.75, f2 = -1.23;
float res;

int main(void)
{
  res = add2fp(f1, f2);
  printf("Sum = %f\n", res);
  return 0;
}
```

The application produces the following output:

Sum = -1.980000

Example 2

In this example, the assembly function **add2fpp** (**Listing 3**) is designed to add two single-precision floating-point numbers whose addresses are passed in **r0** and **r1**. It differs from the previous examples in that it's working with pointers to floats rather than the float values directly.

The function expects:

- **r0** to contain the address of the first float.
- **r1** to contain the address of the second float.

It then:

- Loads both float values from memory into s0 and s1 using the instructions

  vldr.f32 s0, [r0]
  vldr.f32 s1, [r1]

- Adds them together (instruction ` **vadd.f32 s0, s1**`).
- Leaves the result in **s0**, which is where the calling function expects to find the return value for a float.

This approach might be used when working with arrays of floats or when passing floats by reference. It's a bit more flexible than the direct register-to-register approach we saw earlier, as it can work with float values stored in memory.

Listing 3.

```
.syntax unified
.cpu cortex-m4
.thumb
.type add2fpp, %function
.global add2fpp
.section .text
add2fpp:
  vldr.f32 s0, [r0]
  vldr.f32 s1, [r1]
  vadd.f32 s0, s1
  bx lr
```

The C code that calls the function **add2fpp** is shown in **Listing 4**.

Listing 4.

```c
#include <stdio.h>

extern float add2fpp(float *f1, float *f2);

float f1 = -82.11, f2 = -101.04;
float res;

int main(void)
{
    res = add2fpp(&f1, &f2);
    printf("Sum = %6.3f\n", res);
    return 0;
}
```

The application produces the following output:

Sum = -183.150

Example 3

It is easily to modify the **add2fpp** function (see **Listing 3**) to return the address of the result instead of the direct value. Here's the modified version named **add2f_ptr** (**Listing 5**).

Listing 5.

```
.syntax unified
.cpu cortex-m4
.thumb
.type add2f_ptr, %function
.global add2f_ptr
.section .text
add2f_ptr:
    vldr.f32 s0, [r0]        // Load first float from address in r0
    vldr.f32 s1, [r1]        // Load second float from address in r1
    vadd.f32 s2, s0, s1      // Add the two floats, result in s2
    vstr.f32 s2, [r2]        // Store result at address in r2
    mov r0, r2              // Move result address to r0 for return
```

```
bx lr              // Return
```

Let's break down the changes and explain how this modified version works:
The function now expects three parameters:
- **r0**: Address of the first float
- **r1**: Address of the second float
- **r2**: Address where the result should be stored

1. **vldr.f32 s0, [r0]** and **vldr.f32 s1, [r1]**: These remain the same, loading the input floats from memory.
2. **vadd.f32 s2, s0, s1**: The addition result is now stored in **s2** instead of **s0**.
3. **vstr s2, [r2]**: This new instruction stores the result (from **s2**) at the memory address provided in **r2**.
4. **mov r0, r2**: This moves the address of the result (which is in **r2**) to **r0**. In ARM calling convention, **r0** is used for returning values, so this effectively returns the address of the result.
5. **bx lr**: This returns from the function as before.

To call the function **add2f_ptr** from C, we might use the following code (**Listing 6**).

Listing 6.

```
#include <stdio.h>

extern float* add2f_ptr(float *f1, float *f2, float *res);

float f1 = -122.07, f2 = -71.08;
float res;
float* res_ptr = &res;

int main(void)
{
 res_ptr = add2f_ptr(&f1, &f2, res_ptr);
 printf("Sum = %6.3f\n", *res_ptr);
 return 0;
}
```

The application produces the following output:

Sum = -193.150

Example 4

In this example, the assembly function **sub2fpp** performs the subtraction of two single-precision floating point numbers (**Listing 7**).

Listing 7.

```
.syntax unified
.cpu cortex-m4
.thumb
.type sub2fpp, %function
.global sub2fpp
.section .text
sub2fpp:
    vldr.f32 s0, [r0]      // Load first float from address in r0
    vldr.f32 s1, [r1]      // Load second float from address in r1
    vsub.f32 s0, s1    // Subtract the two floats, result in s2
    bx lr                // Return
```

The C code that calls the **sub2fpp** function is shown in **Listing 8**.

Listing 8.

```
#include <stdio.h>

extern float sub2fpp(float *f1, float *f2);

float f1 = -22.36, f2 = -71.24;
float res;

int main(void)
{
res = sub2fpp(&f1, &f2);
printf("Difference = %6.3f\n", res);
return 0;
}
```

The application produces the following output:

Difference = 48.880

Example 5

Here's the assembly function **max_float** (**Listing 9**) to find the maximum of two single-precision floating-point numbers and return the result to a C caller, compatible with Cortex-M4.

Listing 9.

```
.syntax unified
.cpu cortex-m4
.thumb
.global max_float
.type max_float, %function
.section .text
max_float:
    vcmp.f32 s0, s1     // Compare s0 (first argument) with s1
                        // (second argument)
    vmrs APSR_nzcv, FPSCR  // Move floating-point status to
                           // ARM status register
    ite ge                   // If s0 >= s1
    vmovge.f32 s0, s0    // Then move s0 to s0 (no change, s0 is larger)
    vmovlt.f32 s0, s1    // Else move s1 to s0 (s1 is larger)
    bx lr                // Return to caller
```

This code assumes the following:
1. The Cortex-M4 is configured to use the FPU (Floating-Point Unit).
2. The two float arguments are passed in **s0** and **s1** registers.
3. The result is returned in **s0**.

The C code that calls the **max_float** function looks like the following (**Listing 10**).

Listing 10.

```
#include <stdio.h>
```

```c
// Declare the assembly function
extern float max_float(float a, float b);

int main() {
    float a = -133.4;
    float b = -65.88;
    float result = max_float(a, b);
    printf("The maximum value is: %f\n", result);
    return 0;
}
```

To use this function **max_float** from C, we declare it as:

```c
extern float max_float(float a, float b);
```

Example 6

In this example, we will modify the assembly function **max_float** to find the minimum of two single-precision floating-point numbers and return the result to a C caller. The function named **min_float** is shown in **Listing 11**.

Listing 11.

```
.syntax unified
.cpu cortex-m4
.thumb
.global min_float
.type min_float, %function
.section .text
min_float:
    vcmp.f32 s0, s1        // Compare s0 (first argument) with s1
                           //(second argument)
    vmrs APSR_nzcv, FPSCR  // Move floating-point status
                           // to ARM status register
    ite lt                 // If s0 < s1
    vmovlt.f32 s0, s0      // Then move s0 to s0 (no change, s0 is larger)
    vmovge.f32 s0, s1      // Else move s1 to s0 (s1 is larger)
    bx lr                  // Return to caller
```

173

The C code that calls the assembly function **min_float** looks like the following (**Listing 12**).

Listing 12.

```
#include <stdio.h>

// Declare the assembly function
extern float min_float(float a, float b);

int main() {
    float a = -133.4;
    float b = -165.88;
    float result = min_float(a, b);
    printf("The minimum value is: %f\n", result);
    return 0;
}
```

To use this function **min_float** from C, we declare it as:

```
extern float min_float(float a, float b);
```

Example 7

Here's an assembly function **array_sum** (**Listing 13**) that calculates the sum of a floating-point array.
This function expects:
- **r0**: The address of the float array.
- **r1**: The size of the array (number of elements).

It returns the sum in **s0**, which is where C code expects to find a floating-point return value.

Listing 13.

```
.syntax unified
.cpu cortex-m4
.thumb
```

```
.global array_sum
.type array_sum, %function
.section .text
array_sum:
    vsub.f32 s0, s0      // Initialize sum to 0
    mov r2, #0           // Initialize counter to 0
loop:
    cmp r2, r1           // Compare counter with array size
    bge end              // If counter >= size, exit loop
    vldr.f32 s1, [r0]        // Load array element into s1
    vadd.f32 s0, s0, s1  // Add element to sum
    add r0, r0, #4       // Move to next array element (4 bytes per float)
    add r2, r2, #1       // Increment counter
    b loop               // Continue loop
end:
    bx lr                // Return to caller
```

Let's break down this code:

1. We use the appropriate directives for Cortex-M4 with floating-point support.
2. The function **array_sum** is defined and made global.
3. `vsub.f32 s0, s0` initializes our sum to 0.
4. `mov r2, #0` initializes our loop counter.
5. The **loop** label starts our main loop:
    - The code compares the counter (**r2**) with the array size (**r1**).
    - If the counter is greater than or equal to the size, the code jumps to **end**.
    - Otherwise, the current array element is loaded into **s1**.
    - The code adds this element to our running sum in **s0**.
    - Then the array pointer (**r0**) is incremented by 4 bytes (size of a float).
    - The counter (**r2**) is incremented by 1.
    - The code branches back to the start of the loop.
6. When the loop is done, the function returns to the caller with `bx lr`.

The C code that calls the function **array_sum** is shown in **Listing 14**.

Listing 14.

```c
#include <stdio.h>

extern float array_sum(float* array, int size);
float my_array[5] = {1.1, 2.2, 3.3, 4.4, 5.5};

int main()
{
  float sum = array_sum(my_array, 5);
  printf("Sum = %6.3f\n", sum);
  return 0;
}
```

The application produces the following output:

Sum = 16.500

Example 8

Below (**Listing 15**) is the assembly function **array_max** that finds the maximum element in a single-precision floating-point array.
This function expects:

- **r0**: The address of the float array
- **r1**: The size of the array (number of elements)

It returns the maximum value in **s0**, which is where C code expects to find a floating-point return value.

Listing 15.

```
.syntax unified
.cpu cortex-m4
.thumb
.global array_max
.type array_max, %function
.section .text
array_max:
    vldr.f32 s0, [r0]       // Load first element as initial max
    mov r2, #1              // Initialize counter to 1 (we've already loaded the
```

```
                        // first element)

loop:
    cmp r2, r1          // Compare counter with array size
    bge end             // If counter >= size, exit loop

    add r0, r0, #4          // Move to next array element (4 bytes per float)
    vldr.f32 s1, [r0]           // Load current array element into s1
    vcmp.f32 s1, s0             // Compare current element with max
    vmrs APSR_nzcv, FPSCR   //Move floating-point flags to ARM flags
    ble no_update           // If current <= max, don't update
    vmov.f32 s0, s1         // Update max

no_update:
    add r2, r2, #1          // Increment counter
    b loop                  // Continue loop

end:
    bx lr                   //Return to caller
```

Let's break down this code:

1. We use the appropriate directives for Cortex-M4 with floating-point support.
2. The function **array_max** is defined and made global.
3. `vldr.f32 s0, [r0]` loads the first element of the array as our initial maximum.
4. `mov r2, #1` initializes our loop counter to 1 (since we've already loaded the first element).
5. The **loop** label starts our main loop:
    • The counter (**r2**) is compared with the array size (**r1**).
    • If the counter is greater than or equal to the size, the code jumps to **end**.
    • Otherwise, we move to the next array element and load it into **s1**.
    • The current element (**s1**) is then compared with our current max (**s0**).
    • The instruction `vmrs APSR_nzcv, FPSCR` is used to transfer the floating-point comparison flags to the ARM flags.
    • If the current element is less than or equal to the max, the code skips the update.

- If it's greater, the max in **s0** is updated.
- The counter (**r2**) is then updated and the loop continues.
6. When the loop is done, the function returns to the caller with `bx lr`.

The C code that calls the function **array_max** looks like the following (**Listing 16**).

Listing 16.

```
#include <stdio.h>

extern float array_max(float* array, int size);
float my_array[5] = {-31.29, -152.48, -103.03, -75.11, -95.27};

int main()
{
  float max_val = array_max(my_array, 5);
  printf("Maximum = %6.3f\n", max_val);
  return 0;
}
```

The application produces the following output:

Maximum = -31.290

Example 9

It is easily to modify the assembly function **array_max** to search for the minimum in a single-precision floating point array. The modified assembly function named **array_min** is shown in **Listing 17**.

Listing 17.

```
.syntax unified
.cpu cortex-m4
.thumb
.global array_min
```

```
.type array_min, %function
.section .text
array_min:
    vldr.f32 s0, [r0]        // Load first element as initial max
    mov r2, #1               // Initialize counter to 1 (we've already loaded the
                             // first element)
loop:
    cmp r2, r1               // Compare counter with array size
    bge end                  // If counter >= size, exit loop

    add r0, r0, #4           // Move to next array element (4 bytes per float)
    vldr.f32 s1, [r0]        // Load current array element into s1
    vcmp.f32 s1, s0          // Compare current element with max
    vmrs APSR_nzcv, FPSCR   // Move floating-point flags to ARM flags
    it  le                   // If current >= min, don't update
    vmovle.f32 s0, s1        // Update min
    add r2, r2, #1           // Increment counter
    b loop                   // Continue loop
end:
    bx lr                    // Return to caller
```

The C code that calls the function **array_min** looks like the following (**Listing 18**).

Listing 18.

```
#include <stdio.h>

extern float array_min(float* array, int size);
float my_array[5] = {-231.29, -152.48, -103.03, -75.11, -945.27};

int main()
{
  float min_val = array_min(my_array, 5);
  printf("Minimum = %6.3f\n", min_val);
  return 0;
}
```

The application produces thr following output:

179

Minimum = -945.270

Example 10

In this example (**Listing 19**), the assembly function **abs_float_array** converts each element of a 5-element single-precision floating-point array into the corresponding absolute value.

Listing 19.

```
.syntax unified
.cpu cortex-m4
.thumb
.global abs_float_array
.section .text
abs_float_array:
    push {r4, lr}
loop:
    vldr.f32 s0, [r0]    // Load float from memory into s0
    vabs.f32 s0, s0      // Compute absolute value
    vstr.f32 s0, [r0]    // Store result back to memory
    adds r0, r0, #4      // Move to next float (4 bytes)
    subs r1, r1, #1      // Decrement counter
    bne loop             // If counter != 0, continue loop
    pop {r4, pc}
```

Explanation:
1. The **abs_float_array** function starts by pushing **r4** and **lr** onto the stack (though **r4** isn't used in this simple example, it's included for demonstration).
2. **r0** is assumed to contain the address of the float9ng-point array.
3. **r1** is assumed to contain the size of the array (=5), which will be our loop counter.
4. The main **loop**:
    - Loads a float from memory into **s0** using `vldr.f32`.
    - Computes the absolute value using `vabs.f32`
    - Stores the result back to memory using `vstr.f32`.
    - Increments the array pointer by 4 bytes (size of a float).

- Decrements the counter.
- Continues if the counter is not zero.

5. Finally, it restores **r4** and **lr** from the stack and returns.

This code modifies the array in-place, replacing each element with its absolute value.

The C code that calls the function **abs_float_array** is shown in **Listing 20**.

Listing 20.

```c
#include <stdio.h>

extern void abs_float_array(float *pf1, int asize);
float a1[5] = { -4.98, 1.66, 3.09, -51.54, 7.11 };

int main()
{
  abs_float_array(a1, 5);
  for (int i1 = 0; i1 < 5; i1++)
    printf("%6.3f\n", a1[i1]);
  return 0;
}
```

Example 11

In this example, the assembly function **find_first_negative** (**Listing 21**) searches for the first negative element in a 5-element single-precision floating-point array and returns the index of this element (if found) or -1 if nothing found.

Listing 21.

```
.syntax unified
.cpu cortex-m4
.thumb
.global find_first_negative
.section .text
```

181

```
find_first_negative:
    push {r4, lr}
    movs r2, #0        // Initialize index counter to 0
    vsub.f32 s1, s1    // Load 0.0 into s1 for comparison

loop:
    vldr.f32 s0, [r0]   // Load float from memory into s0
    vcmp.f32 s0, s1     // Compare float with 0.0
    vmrs APSR_nzcv, FPSCR // Move floating-point status to APSR
    blt found           // If less than 0, branch to found
    adds r0, r0, #4     // Move to next float (4 bytes)
    adds r2, r2, #1     // Increment index counter
    subs r1, r1, #1     // Decrement loop counter
    bne loop            // If loop counter != 0, continue loop

    movs r0, #-1        // If loop completed, return -1
    pop {r4, pc}

found:
    mov r0, r2         // Move index to r0 (return value)
    pop {r4, pc}
```

Here's an explanation of the code:

1. We push **r4** and **lr** onto the stack (though **r4** isn't used in this example, it's included for demonstration).
2. **r0** is assumed to contain the address of the float array.
3. **r1** is assumed to be the size of the array (=5).
4. **r2** will be the index counter (set to 0).
5. The value **0.0** is loaded into **s1** for comparison (instruction **vsub.f32 s1, s1**).
6. The main **loop**:
   - Loads a float from memory into **s0** using `vldr.f32`.
   - Compares the float with **0.0** using `vcmp.f32`.
   - Moves the floating-point status to APSR.
   - If the float is less than **0.0**, branches to **found**.
   - If not, it increments the array pointer and index, decrements the loop counter.
   - Continues if the loop counter is not zero.
7. If the loop completes without finding a negative number, **r0** is set to -1 and the function returns.

8. If a negative number is found, the current index (**r2**) is moved to **r0** as the return value.
9. Finally, it restores **r4** and **lr** from the stack and returns.

The C code that calls the function **find_first_negative** is shown in **Listing 22**.

Listing 22.

```
#include <stdio.h>

extern int find_first_negative(float *pf1, int asize);
float a1[5] = { 4.98, -1.66, 3.09, 51.54, 7.11 };

int main()
{
    int ind = find_first_negative(a1, 5);
    printf("Index of a first negative element: %d\n", ind);
    return 0;
}
```

The application produces the following output:

Index of a first negative element: 1

Example 12

We can optimize the code of the function **find_first_negative** using an IT-block. The modified version of this function is shown in **Listing 23**.

Listing 23.

```
.syntax unified
.cpu cortex-m4
.thumb
.global find_first_negative
.section .text
find_first_negative:
    push {r4, lr}
```

```
    movs r2, #0        // Initialize index counter to 0
    vsub.f32 s1, s1    // Load 0.0 into s1 for comparison

loop:
    vldr.f32 s0, [r0]    // Load float from memory into s0
    vcmp.f32 s0, s1      // Compare float with 0.0
    vmrs APSR_nzcv, FPSCR // Move floating-point status to APSR
    itt lt
    movlt r0, r2
    poplt {r4, pc}

    adds r0, r0, #4    // Move to next float (4 bytes)
    adds r2, r2, #1    // Increment index counter
    subs r1, r1, #1    // Decrement loop counter
    bne loop           // If loop counter != 0, continue loop

    movs r0, #-1       // If loop completed, return -1
    pop {r4, pc}
```

Code Analysis with IT Block:

1. **Comparison of the Floating-Point Number**:
   - We compare **s0** (the loaded float) with **s1**, which holds **0.0** via `vcmp.f32 s0, s1` and move the result to the **APSR** register using `vmrs APSR_nzcv, FPSCR`. This sets the condition flags (Negative, Zero, Carry, Overflow).
2. **Conditional Execution (IT block)**:
   - The `itt lt` block sets up two subsequent instructions to be conditionally executed if the `less than` (negative flag) condition is met. This will only happen if the value in **s0** is less than zero.
   - **movlt r0, r2**: If the condition is met, it moves the index (in **r2**) to **r0**, preparing to return the index.
   - **poplt {r4, pc}**: If the condition is met, it also pops **r4** and **pc**, effectively returning from the function.
3. **Loop Continuation**:
   - If the condition is not met (i.e., the value in **s0** is not less than zero), the IT block is skipped, and the next instructions continue as normal:
   - We increment **r0** (move to the next float).

- We increment **r2** (update the index counter).
- We decrement **r1** (check the remaining elements).
- If **r1** != 0, we branch back to loop and continue checking the next element.
4. **End of Loop**: If the loop completes without finding any negative values, we return -1 by moving -1 to **r0** and popping the registers.

Example 13

In this example, the assembly function **find_first_positive (Listing 24)** searches for the first positive element in a 5-element single-precision floating-point array and returns the index of this element (if found) or -1 if nothing found. The function takes 2 parameters, the address of an array (**r0**) and the size of the array (**r1**).

Listing 24.

```
.syntax unified
.cpu cortex-m4
.thumb
.global find_first_positive
.section .text
find_first_positive:
    push {r4, lr}
    movs r2, #0        // Initialize index counter to 0
    vsub.f32 s1, s1    // Load 0.0 into s1 for comparison

loop:
    vldr.f32 s0, [r0]   // Load float from memory into s0
    vcmp.f32 s0, s1     // Compare float with 0.0
    vmrs APSR_nzcv, FPSCR // Move floating-point status to APSR
    itt ge
    movge r0, r2
    popge {r4, pc}

    adds r0, r0, #4     // Move to next float (4 bytes)
    adds r2, r2, #1     // Increment index counter
    subs r1, r1, #1     // Decrement loop counter
```

```
    bne loop          // If loop counter != 0, continue loop

    movs r0, #-1      // If loop completed, return -1
    pop {r4, pc}
```

The C code that calls the function **find_first_positive** is shown below (**Listing 25**).

Listing 25.

```
#include <stdio.h>

extern int find_first_positive(float *pf1, int asize);
float a1[5] = { -4.98, 1.66, -3.09, 51.54, -7.11 };

int main()
{
  int ind = find_first_positive(a1, 5);
  printf("Index of a first positive element: %d\n", ind);
  return 0;
}
```

The application produces the following output:

Index of a first positive element: 1

Example 14

Tis example illustrates one more optimization method using the IT-block for the assembler function **find_first_positive** (**Listing 26**).

Listing 26.

```
.syntax unified
.cpu cortex-m4
.thumb
.global find_first_positive
.section .text
find_first_positive:
```

```
    push {r4, lr}
    movs r2, #0      // Initialize index counter to 0
    vsub.f32 s1, s1  // Load 0.0 into s1 for comparison

loop:
    vldr.f32 s0, [r0]   // Load float from memory into s0
    vcmp.f32 s0, s1     // Compare float with 0.0
    vmrs APSR_nzcv, FPSCR // Move floating-point status to APSR
    itt ge
    movge r0, r2
    bge exit

    adds r0, r0, #4     // Move to next float (4 bytes)
    adds r2, r2, #1     // Increment index counter
    subs r1, r1, #1     // Decrement loop counter
    bne loop            // If loop counter != 0, continue loop

    movs r0, #-1        // If loop completed, return -1
exit:
    pop {r4, pc}
```

Let's consider the following key points:

1. The `vcmp.f32` instruction compares **s0** (the current floating-point value loaded from the array) with **s1** (which has **0.0**).

2. The result of the comparison is stored in the **FPSCR** (Floating Point Status Control Register), and `vmrs` transfers these flags into the **APSR**.

3. After the comparison and flag transfer, the IT block begins. If the condition `ge` (greater than or equal) is true, both the `movge r0, r2` (updating **r0** to the current index) and `bge exit` (branching to exit) will execute.

Example 15

In this example, the assembly function **compare_float_arrays (Listing 27)** compares two 5-element single-precision floating-point arrays and returns the number of mismatched elements.

Listing 27.

```
.syntax unified
.cpu cortex-m4
.thumb
.global compare_float_arrays
.section .text
compare_float_arrays:
    PUSH    {LR}                    // Save the return address
    MOVS    R2, #0                  // R2 will count the mismatches
    MOVS    R3, #5                  // Loop counter set to 5 elements

compare_loop:
    VLDR.F32    S0, [R0]            // Load element from the first array
    VLDR.F32    S1, [R1]            // Load element from the second array
    VCMPE.F32 S0, S1                // Compare the two floating-point values
    VMRS    APSR_nzcv, FPSCR        // Move FPSCR flags to APSR
    BNE     mismatch_found          // If not equal, branch to mismatch

    // If equal, proceed to the next elements
    ADD     R0, R0, #4              // Move to the next element in the first array
    ADD     R1, R1, #4              // Move to the next element in the second
                                    // array
    SUBS    R3, R3, #1              // Decrement loop counter
    BNE     compare_loop            // If counter is not zero, continue loop

    // No mismatches found, return the result
    B       done

mismatch_found:
    ADDS    R2, R2, #1              // Increment the mismatch counter
    ADD     R0, R0, #4              // Move to the next element in the first array
    ADD     R1, R1, #4              // Move to the next element in the second
                                    // array
    SUBS    R3, R3, #1              // Decrement loop counter
    BNE     compare_loop            // If counter is not zero, continue loop

done:
    MOV     R0, R2                  // Move the mismatch count to R0 (return
                                    // value)
```

```
POP    {PC}              // Return to the caller
```

Explanation

1. The assembly code compares each element of the two arrays. If the elements differ, it increments a mismatch counter (**R2**).
2. The comparison uses the `VCMPE.F32` instruction, which is a floating-point comparison specific to the Cortex-M4.
3. After the loop, the function returns the mismatch count in register **R0** to the caller.

The C code that calls the **compare_float_arrays** function looks like the following (**Listing 28**).

Listing 28.

```
#include <stdio.h>

extern int compare_float_arrays(float *arr1, float *arr2);

int main() {
    float array1[5] = {1.01, 2.11, 3.19, -4.06, 5.1};
    float array2[5] = {-1.03, 2.11, 3.17, -4.07, 5.1};
    int mismatches = compare_float_arrays(array1, array2);
    printf("Number of mismatches: %d\n", mismatches);
    return 0;
}
```

The application produces the following output:

Number of mismatches: 3

Example 16

Here's an assembly function **count_in_range** (**Listing 29**) that counts the number of elements in the range ([-5, 5]) in a 5-element single-precision floating-point array. The values -5.0 and 5.0 will be counted as well.

Listing 29.

```
.syntax unified
.cpu cortex-m4
.thumb
.global count_in_range
.section .data
    array: .float 1.14, 5.0, 3.5, 14.2, -5.0  // Example array
.section .text
count_in_range:
    PUSH   {LR}              // Save return address
    LDR    R1, =array        // Load address of the array
    MOV    R2, #0            // Initialize counter to 0
    MOV    R3, #5            // Number of elements in the array
    VMOV.F32 S1, #-5.0
    VMOV.F32 S2, #5.0

loop:
    VLDR.F32   S0, [R1]       // Load array element into S0
    VCMPE.F32 S0, S1         // Compare element with -5.0
    VMRS   APSR_nzcv, FPSCR   // Move FPSCR to APSR
    BLT    out_of_range       // If element < -5, skip increment

    VCMPE.F32 S0, S2          // Compare element with 5.0
    VMRS   APSR_nzcv, FPSCR   // Move FPSCR to APSR
    BGT    out_of_range       // If element > 5, skip increment

    ADD    R2, R2, #1        // Increment counter

out_of_range:
    ADD    R1, R1, #4        // Move to the next element
    SUBS   R3, R3, #1        // Decrement loop counter
    BNE    loop              // If not done, repeat loop

    MOV    R0, R2            // Move counter to R0 (return value)
    POP    {LR}              // Restore return address
    BX     LR                // Return from function
```

This code initializes a counter, iterates through the array, and checks if each element is within the specified range. If an element is within the range, it increments the counter. Finally, it returns the count.

The C code that calls the function **count_in_range** is shown in **Listing 30**.

Listing 30.

```
#include <stdio.h>

extern int count_in_range(void);

int main() {
    int num_in_range = count_in_range();
    printf("Number of elements in the range [-5, 5] : %d\n", num_in_range);
    return 0;
}
```

The application produces the following output:

Number of elements in the range [-5, 5] : 4

Example 17

This example shows a modified version of the assembly function **count_in_range** from the previous example. This function now takes 2 parameters, the address of the array (**r0**) and the size of this array (**r1**). The modified assembly function code is shown in **Listing 31**. The values -5.0 and 5.0 will be counted as well.

Listing 31.

```
.syntax unified
.cpu cortex-m4
.thumb
.global count_in_range
.section .text
count_in_range:
    MOV    R3, #0          // Initialize counter to 0
```

```
MOV     R4, #5          // Number of elements in the array
VMOV.F32 S1, #-5.0
VMOV.F32 S2, #5.0

loop:
    VLDR.F32    S0, [R0]        // Load array element into S0
    VCMPE.F32 S0, S1            // Compare element with -5.0
    VMRS    APSR_nzcv, FPSCR    // Move FPSCR to APSR
    BLT     out_of_range        // If element < -5, skip increment

    VCMPE.F32 S0, S2            // Compare element with 5.0
    VMRS    APSR_nzcv, FPSCR    // Move FPSCR to APSR
    BGT     out_of_range        // If element > 5, skip increment

    ADD     R3, R3, #1          // Increment counter

out_of_range:
    ADD     R0, R0, #4          // Move to the next element
    SUBS    R4, R4, #1          // Decrement loop counter
    BNE     loop                // If not done, repeat loop

    MOV     R0, R3          // Move counter to R0 (return value)
    BX      LR              // Return from function
```

The C code that calls the function **count_in_range** looks like the following (**Listing 32**).

Listing 32.

```
#include <stdio.h>

extern int count_in_range(float *pf, int asize);
float a1[5] = {5.2, -2.11, 3.09, -8.06, -4.99};

int main() {
  int num_in_range = count_in_range(a1, 5);
  printf("Number of elements in the range [-5, 5] : %d\n", num_in_range);
  return 0;
}
```

The application produces the following output:

Number of elements in the range [-5, 5] : 3

Example 18

In this example, the assembly function **count_outside_range** (**Listing 33**) counts the number of elements outside the range ([-5, 5]) in a 5-element single-precision floating-point array. This function takes 2 parameters, the address of the array (**r0**) and the size of this array (**r1**).

Listing 33.

```
.syntax unified
.cpu cortex-m4
.thumb
.global count_outside_range
.section .text
count_outside_range:
    MOV    R3, #0              // Initialize counter to 0
    MOV    R4, #5              // Number of elements in the array
    VMOV.F32 S1, #-5.0         // Load -5.0 into S1
    VMOV.F32 S2, #5.0          // Load 5.0 into S2

loop:
    VLDR.F32   S0, [R0]        // Load array element into S0
    VCMPE.F32 S0, S1           // Compare element with -5.0
    VMRS    APSR_nzcv, FPSCR   // Move FPSCR to APSR
    BLT    increment_counter   // If element < -5, increment counter

    VCMPE.F32 S0, S2           // Compare element with 5.0
    VMRS    APSR_nzcv, FPSCR   // Move FPSCR to APSR
    BGT    increment_counter   // If element > 5, increment counter

inc_address:
    ADD    R0, R0, #4          // Move to the next element
    SUBS   R4, R4, #1          // Decrement loop counter
    BNE    loop                // If not done, repeat loop
```

```
    MOV    R0, R3          // Move counter to R0 (return value)
    BX     LR              // Return from function

increment_counter:
    ADD    R3, R3, #1       // Increment counter
    B      inc_address      // Jump to address increment and loop decrement
```

The C code that calls the function **count_outside_range** looks like the following (**Listing 34**).

Listing 34.

```
#include <stdio.h>

extern int count_outside_range(float *fa1, int asize);
float a1[5] = {5.01, -1.11, 10.09, -22.06, -5.04};

int main() {
    int num = count_outside_range(a1, 5);
    printf("Number of elements outside the range [-5, 5] : %d\n", num);
    return 0;
}
```

The application produces the following output:

Number of elements outside the range [-5, 5] : 4

Example 19

We can easily optimize the assembly function **count_outside_range** using the IT-block. Using the IT (If-Then) block is a great way to conditionally execute instructions in Thumb mode on Cortex-M processors. The IT block improves the efficiency by reducing the number of branch instructions. The modified version of function **count_outside_range** is shown in **Listing 35**.

Listing 35.

```
.syntax unified
.cpu cortex-m4
```

```
.thumb
.global count_outside_range
.section .text
count_outside_range:
    MOV    R3, #0          // Initialize counter to 0
    MOV    R4, #5          // Number of elements in the array
    VMOV.F32 S1, #-5.0     // Load -5.0 into S1
    VMOV.F32 S2, #5.0      // Load 5.0 into S2

loop:
    VLDR.F32   S0, [R0]        // Load array element into S0
    VCMPE.F32 S0, S1          // Compare element with -5.0
    VMRS    APSR_nzcv, FPSCR   // Move FPSCR to APSR
    IT    LT
    ADDLT  R3, R3, #1
    VCMPE.F32 S0, S2          // Compare element with 5.0
    VMRS    APSR_nzcv, FPSCR   // Move FPSCR to APSR
    IT    GT
    ADDGT   R3, R3, #1

    ADD    R0, R0, #4      // Move to the next element
    SUBS   R4, R4, #1      // Decrement loop counter
    BNE    loop            // If not done, repeat loop

    MOV    R0, R3          // Move counter to R0 (return value)
    BX     LR              // Return from function
```

Analysis:

- **VCMPE.F32 S0, S1**: Compares the floating-point value in **S0** with $-5.0-5.0-5.0$.
- **IT LT / ADDLT R3, R3, #1**: If the result of the comparison is "less than" (LT), then **R3** is incremented.
- **VCMPE.F32 S0, S2**: Compares the floating-point value in **S0** with $5.05.05.0$.
- **IT GT / ADDGT R3, R3, #1**: If the result of the comparison is "greater than" (GT), then R3 is incremented.
- **Remaining code**: Unconditionally increments the address and decrements the loop counter, as in previous versions.

Example 20

In this example, we will calculate the **Mean**, often referred to as the average, is a measure of central tendency that summarizes a set of data by identifying the central point within that dataset. It is calculated by adding up all the values in the dataset and then dividing by the number of values.

Formula for the Mean μ for a dataset with values $(x_1, x_2, \ldots, x_n)$ is calculated as:

$$\mu = (x_1 + x_2 + \ldots + x_n) / n$$

For example, suppose we have the following dataset: $(2, 4, 6, 8, 10)$. Calculating the mean gives us

$$\mu = (2 + 4 + 6 + 8 + 10) / 5 = 30 / 5 = 6$$

Applications

The mean is widely used in various fields such as statistics, economics, finance, and general data analysis to provide a simple summary of the data. It helps to understand the overall level of the data and is often used in conjunction with other measures like the **median** and **mode** to get a comprehensive view of the dataset's characteristics.

Here's the Cortex-M4 assembly function **calculate_mean** (**Listing 36**) that calculates the mean of 10 single-precision floating-point elements in an array. The result will be stored in the **s0** register. The array base address is passed in the **r0** register.

Listing 36.

```
.syntax unified
.cpu cortex-m4
.thumb
.global calculate_mean
.type calculate_mean, %function
.section .text
```

```
calculate_mean:
    VSTMDB  SP!, {S1-S2}     // Save registers on stack (if needed)
    MOV  R1, #10             // Set loop count for 10 elements
    VSUB.F32 S1, S1          // S1 will hold the running sum
    MOV  R2, #0              // Initialize index (R2 = 0)

loop:
    VLDR.F32 S2, [R0]        // Load element from the array into S2
    VADD.F32 S1, S1, S2      // Add the element to the running sum in S1
    ADD R0, #4               // Increment address
    ADD R2, #1               // Increment index
    CMP R2, R1               // Compare index with 10
    BLT loop                 // Loop if R2 < 10

    VMOV.F32 S0, #10.0       // Load constant 10.0 into S0
    VDIV.F32 S1, S1, S0      // Divide the sum by 10.0 (S1 / 10.0)
    VMOV S0, S1              // Move the result to S0 (mean)
    VLDMIA  SP!, {S1-S2}     // Restore saved registers
    BX   LR                  // Return from function
```

Explanation:
- The array base address is passed in **r0**.
- **s1** holds the running sum of all elements.
- A loop is used to iterate over the 10 elements in the array, each element is loaded into **s2** and added to the running sum in **s1**.
- After summing the 10 elements, the final sum is divided by 10 to calculate the mean.
- The result (mean) is returned in **s0**.

The C code that call the function **calculate_mean** looks like the following (**Listing 37**).

Listing 37.

```
#include <stdio.h>

// Declaration of the assembly function
extern float calculate_mean(float *array);

int main(void) {
```

```
// Define an array of 10 floating-point numbers
float numbers[10] = {1.0, 2.5, 3.2, 4.0, 5.5, 6.1, 7.0, 8.3, 9.7, 10.4};

// Call the assembly function and get the mean
float mean = calculate_mean(numbers);

// Print the result
printf("The mean of the array is: %f\n", mean);
return 0;
}
```

The application produces the following output:

The mean of the array is: 5.770000

Example 21

In this example, we consider how to calculate RMS using an assembly function **calculate_rms**. RMS stands for Root Mean Square, and it is a statistical measure used to determine the magnitude of a varying quantity. It is especially useful in contexts where both positive and negative values occur, as it provides a measure of the average magnitude irrespective of the sign.

Calculation of RMS

The RMS value of a set of values $x_1, x_2, \ldots, x_n$ is calculated using the following steps:

1. **Square each value.**
2. **Find the mean (average) of these squared values.**
3. **Take the square root of this mean.**

Mathematically, the RMS is given by:

$$RMS = \sqrt{[(x_1^2 + x_2^2 + \cdots + x_n^2)/n]}$$

Example

Consider the dataset: 2, 3, 1, 5, 4.

1. **Square each value:**

$$2^2=4,\ 3^2=9,\ 1^2=1,\ 5^2=25,\ 4^2=16$$

2. **Find the mean of these squared values:**

$$\text{Mean} = (4+9+1+25+16)/5 = 11$$

3. **Take the square root of this mean:**

$$\text{RMS}=\sqrt{11}\approx3.32$$

Applications of RMS

4. **Electrical Engineering**: RMS values are used to calculate the effective value of alternating currents and voltages. For example, the RMS value of an AC voltage is the DC equivalent that would produce the same amount of heat in a resistor.
5. **Signal Processing**: RMS is used to quantify the magnitude of a varying signal. This is particularly useful for audio signals to measure their power.
6. **Statistics**: RMS is used as a measure of the magnitude of a set of values, irrespective of their sign. This is useful in various statistical analyses to describe the overall level of a dataset.
7. **Physics and Engineering**: RMS values are used to describe the average power of mechanical vibrations and waveforms.

Key Points

- RMS provides a single value that represents the magnitude of a set of values.
- It is particularly useful for datasets with both positive and negative values.
- It is widely used in fields where varying quantities are analyzed, such as engineering, physics, and statistics.

The RMS value is a robust measure for analyzing the magnitude of a varying quantity, providing meaningful insights in various practical and theoretical applications.

Let's go to the assembly function **calculate_rms (Listing 38)** that calculates RMS using a 5-element single-precision floating-point array as a dataset.

Listing 38.

```
.syntax unified
.cpu cortex-m4
.thumb
.globl calculate_rms
.type calculate_rms, %function
.section .text
calculate_rms:
    // Input: r0 = address of the array, r1 = size of the array
    movs    r2, #0        // r2 = loop counter (i = 0)
    vsub.f32 s0, s0        // s0 = sum of squares (initialize to 0)
loop:
    cmp     r2, r1        // Compare loop counter with size
    bge     exit          // If counter >= size, exit loop
    vldr.f32 s1, [r0]     // Load float element from array (s1 = array[i])
    vmla.f32 s0, s1, s1   // s0 += s1 * s1 (add square of the element)
    adds    r2, #1        // Increment loop counter (i++)
    adds    r0, #4        // Increment address
    b       loop          // Repeat loop
exit:
    // Calculate the mean of the sum of squares
    vmov.f32 s1, r1       // s1 = size of the array
    vcvt.f32.s32 s1, s1   // convert integer to floating-points1 to
    vdiv.f32 s0, s0, s1   // s0 = sum_of_squares / size

    // Calculate the square root of the mean
    vsqrt.f32 s0, s0      // return s0 = sqrt(mean)
    bx      lr            // Return to the caller
```

Explanation:

1. **Looping Through the Array**: The function iterates over the array, squaring each element and accumulating the sum of squares.
2. **Mean Calculation**: After the loop, the sum of squares is divided by the array size to get the mean of the squares.
3. **Square Root Calculation**: The square root of the mean is computed to give the RMS.
4. **Returning the Result**: The result is returned in register **s0**, as per the ARM calling convention for Cortex-M4.

The C code that calls the function **calculate_rms** looks like the following (**Listing 39**).

Listing 39.

```c
#include <stdio.h>

extern float calculate_rms(float *array, int size);
float a1[5] = { 3.12, -1.55, 0.9, 2.38, 4.01 };

int main()
{
    float rms = calculate_rms(a1, 5);
    printf("RMS = %8.5f\n", rms);
    return 0;
}
```

The application produces the following output:

RMS = 2.63406

Processing double-precision floating-point numbers

In this section, we will consider the operations with double-precision floating point numbers implemented in an ARM Assembly Language.
ARM processors that support operations with double-precision floating-point values include:

1. **ARM11** series: Some later models in this series introduced support for double-precision operations.

2. **Cortex-A** series: Most Cortex-A processors support double-precision operations, from early models like Cortex-A8 to more recent ones like Cortex-A78 and Cortex-X1.

3. **Cortex-M** series:
   - Cortex-M7 and later high-end M-series processors
   - Some Cortex-M33 and Cortex-M55 implementations

4. **Cortex-R** series: Many Cortex-R processors, especially more recent models.

5. **Neoverse** series: Designed for infrastructure, these processors support double-precision operations.

6. **Many custom ARM-based designs** by companies like Apple, Qualcomm, and Samsung also support double-precision operations.

It's important to note that support can vary based on specific implementations and configurations chosen by chip manufacturers. For the most accurate information on a particular processor or SoC (System on Chip), it's best to consult the specific technical documentation provided by the manufacturer.
All examples in this section are based on Cortex-A53 that supports FP-ARMv8 floating-point architecture within the ARMv8-A instruction set, which includes support for advanced SIMD (Single Instruction, Multiple Data) and floating-point operations. This architecture is designed to enhance the performance of floating-point calculations, which are crucial for many scientific, engineering, and multimedia applications.

FP-ARMv8 does support double-precision floating-point operations. The ARMv8-A architecture, which includes the FP-ARMv8 floating-point unit, supports both single-precision (32-bit) and double-precision (64-bit) floating-point arithmetic. This capability is crucial for applications that require high precision and accuracy in numerical computations.

The Cortex-A53 processor, which implements the ARMv8-A architecture, can efficiently handle double-precision floating-point operations thanks to its VFPv4 Floating Point Unit (FPU). This makes it well-suited for tasks such as scientific computing, financial modeling, and any other applications that demand precise and complex mathematical calculations.

Let's consider a few examples where double-precision numbers are involved.

Example 1

In this example, the Cortex-A53 assembly function **reverse_sign_double** (**Listing 1**) reverses the sign of a double-precision floating-point number.

Listing 1.

```
.syntax unified
.cpu cortex-a53
.global reverse_sign_double
.type reverse_sign_double, %function
.section .text
reverse_sign_double:
    // Load the double-precision value into a VFP register
    vldr.f64 d0, [r0]    // Load double from memory pointed by r0 into d0

    // Reverse the sign
    vneg.f64 d0, d0      // Negate d0, result stored back in d0

    // Result is now in d0, which is where C expects it
    // for a double return value
    bx lr                // Return to caller
```

This code does the following:
1. It loads the input double-precision number from the memory location pointed to by **r0** into the VFP register **d0**.

2. It uses the **vneg.f64** instruction to negate the value in **d0**, effectively reversing its sign.
3. The result is left in **d0**, which is where the C ABI expects double-precision return values.

A few notes:

- This code uses VFP (Vector Floating Point) instructions, which are supported by Cortex-A53.
- The **vldr.f64** instruction is used to load the 64-bit (double-precision) value into the VFP register.
- The **vneg.f64** instruction performs the sign reversal operation.
- This operation only changes the sign bit of the floating-point number, leaving the magnitude unchanged.
- When compiling, we need to enable VFP support. With GCC, we might use a flag like `-mfpu=neon-fp-armv8`.

The C caller for the **reverse_sign_double** function looks like the following (**Listing 2**).

Listing 2.

```
#include <stdio.h>
#include <stdlib.h>

extern double reverse_sign_double(double* a);

int main()
{
  double a = 2.47;
  double result = reverse_sign_double(&a);
  printf("Reverse sign value = %f\n", result);
  return 0;
}
```

The application produces the following output:

Reverse sign value = -2.470000

Example 2

Here's the Cortex-A53 assembly function **abs_double** (**Listing 3**) that calculates the absolute value of a double-precision floating-point number:

Listing 3.

```
.syntax unified
.cpu cortex-a53
.global abs_double
.type abs_double, %function
.section .text
abs_double:
    // Load the double-precision value into a VFP register
    vldr.f64 d0, [r0]    // Load double from memory pointed by r0 into d0

    // Calculate absolute value
    vabs.f64 d0, d0      // Absolute value of d0, result stored back in d0

    // Result is now in d0, which is where
    // C expects it for a double return value
    bx lr                // Return to caller
```

This code does the following:
- It loads the input double-precision number from the memory location pointed to by **r0** into the VFP register **d0**.
- The **vldr.f64** instruction loads the 64-bit (double-precision) value into the VFP register.
- The **vabs.f64** instruction calculates the absolute value of the floating-point number.
- The result is left in **d0**, which is where the C ABI expects double-precision return values.
- When compiling, enable VFP support. With GCC, we might use a flag like `-mfpu=neon-fp-armv8`.

This implementation is efficient as it only requires loading the value, performing a single absolute value operation, and returning. The **vabs.f64** instruction handles all the necessary logic to compute the absolute value, including handling special cases like NaN and infinity according to IEEE 754 standards.

The C code that call the **abs_double** function looks like the following (**Listing 4**).

Listing 4.

```c
#include <stdio.h>
#include <stdlib.h>

extern double abs_double(double* a);

int main()
{
    double a = -11.499;
    double result = abs_double(&a);
    printf("Absolute value = %f\n", result);
    return 0;
}
```

The application produces the following output:

Absolute value = 11.499000

Example 3

In this example, the assembly function **max_double** (**Listing 5**) searches for the maximum of two double-precision numbers. The below code will run on Cortex-A53 CPU.

Listing 5.

```asm
.syntax unified
.cpu cortex-a53
.global max_double
.type max_double, %function
.section .text
max_double:
    vcmp.f64 d0, d1              // Compare d0 and d1
```

```
vmrs APSR_nzcv, FPSCR  // Move floating-point status
it lt                  // to ARM status register
vmovlt.f64 d0, d1 // Move d1 to d0 if d1 is greater
bx lr             // Return to caller
```
The C main procedure that calls **max_double** is shown in **Listing 6**.

Listing 6.

```
#include <stdio.h>
#include <stdlib.h>

double d1 = -19.09;
double d2 = -4.44;
double result;

extern double max_double(double d1, double d2);

int main()
{
    result = max_double(d1, d2);
    printf("Maximum = %f\n", result);
    return 0;
}
```

The application produces the following output:

Maximum = -4.440000

Example 4

It is easily to modify the code from **Example 3** in order to find the minimum of two double-precision floating-point numbers. The source code of an assembly procedure **min_double** is shown in **Listing 7**.

Listing 7.

```
.syntax unified
.cpu cortex-a53
.global min_double
```

```
.type min_double, %function
.section .text
min_double:
    vcmp.f64 d0, d1              // Compare d0 and d1
    vmrs APSR_nzcv, FPSCR // Move floating-point status
    it gt                       // to ARM status register
    vmovgt.f64 d0, d1 // Move d1 to d0 if d0 is greater
    bx lr               // Return to caller
```

The C code that calls the **min_double** function is shown in **Listing 8**.

Listing 8.

```
#include <stdio.h>
#include <stdlib.h>

double d1 = -9.09;
double d2 = -18.02;
double result;

extern double min_double(double d1, double d2);

int main()
{
    result = min_double(d1, d2);
    printf("Minimum = %f\n", result);
    return 0;
}
```
The application produces the following output:

Minimum = -18.020000

Example 5

Here's the ARM assembly function **double_add_multiply** (**Listing 9**) for Cortex-A53 that adds two double-precision numbers and then multiplies the sum by a third double-precision number, returning the result to a C caller.

Listing 9.

```
.syntax unified
.cpu cortex-a53
.global double_add_multiply
.type double_add_multiply, %function
.section .text
double_add_multiply:
    // Load the three double-precision values into registers
    vldr.f64 d0, [r0]    // Load first double from memory pointed by r0
    vldr.f64 d1, [r1]    // Load second double from memory pointed by r1
    vldr.f64 d2, [r2]    // Load third double from memory pointed by r2

    // Perform addition
    vadd.f64 d3, d0, d1   // d3 = d0 + d1

    // Perform multiplication
    vmul.f64 d0, d3, d2   // d0 = d3 * d2 (result stored in d0)

    // Result is now in d0, which is
    // where C expects it for a double return value
    bx lr                 // Return to caller
```

This code assumes:

- The three input double-precision numbers are passed in memory locations pointed to by **r0**, **r1**, and **r2**.
- The result is returned in **d0**, which is where C expects a double-precision return value.

A few notes on this code:

1. We use VFP (Vector Floating Point) instructions, which are supported by Cortex-A53.
2. The `vldr.f64` instruction is used to load 64-bit (double-precision) values into the VFP registers.
3. `vadd.f64` and `vmul.f64` perform double-precision addition and multiplication respectively.
4. The final result is left in **d0**, which is where the C ABI expects double-precision return values.

The C code that calls the **double_add_multiply** function is shown in **Listing 10**.

Listing 10.

```c
#include <stdio.h>
#include <stdlib.h>

double a = -11.69;
double b = 2.84;
double c = 14.1;
double result;

extern double double_add_multiply(double* a, double* b, double* c);

int main()
{
    double result = double_add_multiply(&a, &b, &c);
    printf("Result = %f\n", result);
    return 0;
}
```

The application produces the following output:

Result = -124.785000

Example 6

In this example, an assembly function **divide_int_dp** (**Listing 11**) will take two integers as parameters, convert them to double-precision floating-point numbers, perform the division, and return the result to C code.
The procedure will check for division by zero before performing the division. If the denominator is zero, we'll return a special value to indicate an error (in this case, we'll use positive infinity, which is represented as all 1s in the exponent and 0s in the fraction for a 64-bit IEEE 754 double).

Listing 11.

```
.syntax unified
.cpu cortex-a53
.global divide_int_dp
.type divide_int_dp, %function
```

```
.section .text
divide_int_dp:
    // Prologue
    push {r4, lr}

    // Check if denominator (r1) is zero
    cmp r1, #0
    beq divide_by_zero

    // Convert first integer (r0) to double
    vmov s0, r0
    vcvt.f64.s32 d0, s0

    // Convert second integer (r1) to double
    vmov s2, r1
    vcvt.f64.s32 d1, s2

    // Perform division
    vdiv.f64 d0, d0, d1

return:
    // Move result to r0-r1 for return
    vmov r0, r1, d0

    // Epilogue
    pop {r4, pc}

divide_by_zero:
    // Load positive infinity into d0
    vldr.f64 d0, =0x7FF0000000000000
    b return
```

Let's break down this procedure:
1. In the prologue, we push **r4** and **lr** onto the stack. (**r4** isn't used here, but it's common to include it for 8-byte stack alignment).
2. We check to see if the denominator (in r1) is zero:

```
cmp r1, #0
beq divide_by_zero
```

This compares **r1** to 0 and branches to the **divide_by_zero** label if they're equal.

3. We use `vmov` to move the first integer from **r0** to **s0** (a single-precision floating-point register).
4. We convert this integer to a double-precision float using `vcvt.f64.s32`, storing the result in **d0**.
5. We repeat steps 3-4 for the second integer, moving it from **r1** to **s2**, then converting to double-precision in **d1**.
6. We perform the division using `vdiv.f64`, storing the result back in **d0**.
7. We move the result from **d0** to **r0-r1** for return to C code. In ARM EABI, 64-bit values are returned in **r0-r1**.
8. We also introduce a **divide_by_zero** handler:

    vldr.f64 d0, =0x7FF0000000000000
    b return

9. In the epilogue, we pop **r4** and **pc** from the stack, which returns from the function.

Notes

In this procedure, the instruction `vmov r0, r1, d0` on a Cortex-A53 processor is used to transfer data between ARM core registers and NEON/VFP registers. Specifically, this instruction moves the contents of the NEON/VFP register **d0** into the ARM core registers **r0** and **r1**. Here's a breakdown of what happens:

*   The lower 32 bits of the **d0** register are moved into **r0**.
*   The upper 32 bits of the **d0** register are moved into **r1**.

This is useful for operations where you need to manipulate or use the data from NEON/VFP registers in the ARM core registers.

Using the `vmov r0, r1, d0` instruction to return a double-precision value from an assembly procedure to C code is a valid approach. This instruction effectively moves the 64-bit double-precision value from the NEON/VFP register **d0** into the general-purpose registers **r0** and **r1**, which can then be accessed by the C code.

However, it's important to ensure that your calling convention aligns with this method. In the ARM architecture, the AAPCS (ARM Architecture

Procedure Call Standard) specifies that double-precision floating-point values should be returned in the **d0** register. Therefore, if your C code expects the double-precision value to be in **d0**, you might not need to use `vmov` explicitly.

The C code that calls the function **divide_int_dp** looks like the following (**Listing 12**).

Listing 12.

```
#include <stdio.h>
#include <stdlib.h>
#include <math.h>

extern double divide_int_dp(int a1, int a2);

int main()
{
    double result = divide_int_dp(274, 79);
    if (result == INFINITY) {
     printf("Error: Division by zero\n");
    }
    else
    {
     printf("Result: %f\n", result);
    }
  return 0;
}
```

The application produces the following output:

Result: 3.468354

Example 7

In this example, an assembly function **array_sum** (**Listing 13**) calculates the sum of elements in a 5-element double-precision floating-point array.

Listing 13.

```
.syntax unified
.cpu cortex-a53
.global array_sum
.type array_sum, %function
.section .text
array_sum:
    // r0 contains the pointer to the array
    mov r1, #5          // Number of elements
    vsub.f64 d0, d0          // Initialize sum to 0.0

loop:
    vldr.f64 d1, [r0]        // Load double from array
    vadd.f64 d0, d1          // Add to sum
    add r0, r0, #8      // increment a pointer
    subs r1, r1, #1         // Decrement counter
    bne loop               // Continue if not zero

    bx lr                  // Return, sum is in d0
```

The C code that calls the **array_sum** procedure is shown in **Listing 14**.

Listing 14.

```
#include <stdio.h>
#include <stdlib.h>

double a1[5] = { 2.11, -6.09, 2.68, -0.77, 10.29 };
double sum;

extern double array_sum(double * arr);

int main()
{
    sum = array_sum(a1);
    printf("Sum of 5 numbers = %f\n", sum);
    return 0;
}
```

The application produces the following output:

Sum of 5 numbers = 8.220000

Example 8

In this example, the Cortex-A53 assembly function **array_sum_negative** (**Listing 15**) calculates the sum of negative elements in a 5-element double-precision floating-point array.

Listing 15.

```
.syntax unified
.arch armv8-a
.thumb
.global array_sum_negative
.type array_sum_negative, %function
.section .text
array_sum_negative:
    // r0 contains the pointer to the array
    mov r1, #5          // Number of elements
    vsub.f64 d0, d0     // Initialize sum to 0.0
    vsub.f64 d2, d2     // Load 0.0 for comparison

loop:
    vldr.f64 d1, [r0]           // Load double from array
    vcmp.f64 d1, d2             // Compare with 0.0
    vmrs APSR_nzcv, FPSCR       // Move floating-point flags to CPU flags
    bpl skip_add               // Branch if positive or zero
    vadd.f64 d0, d0, d1        // Add to sum if negative
skip_add:
    add r0, r0, #8             // Increment pointer
    subs r1, r1, #1           // Decrement counter
    bne loop                  // Continue if not zero
    bx lr                     // Return, sum is in d0
```

Explanation

1. The instruction `vsub.f64 d2, d2` writes 0.0 into **d2** for comparison.
2. The instruction inside the **loop** do the following:
   - Compare each element with 0.0 using `vcmp.f64 d1, d2`.

- Transfer the floating-point flags to the CPU flags with `vmrs APSR_nzcv, FPSCR`.
- Use `bpl skip_add` to skip the addition if the number is positive or zero.
- Only add the number to the sum if it's negative.

The C code that calls the **array_sum_negative** function looks like the following (**Listing 16**).

Listing 16.

```c
#include <stdio.h>
#include <stdlib.h>

double a1[5] = { -3.19, 6.09, 1.03, -1.77, -6.33 };
double result;

extern double array_sum_negative(double *a1);

int main()
{
  result = array_sum_negative(a1);
  printf("Sum of negatives = %f\n", result);
  return 0;
}
```

The application produces the following output:

Sum of negatives = -11.290000

Example 9

This example illustrates how to optimize the assembly function **array_sum_negative** by excluding the `bpl` branch instruction. The modified assembly code of **array_sum_negative** will then look like the following (**Listing 17**).

Listing 17.

```
.syntax unified
.arch armv8-a
.thumb
.global array_sum_negative
.type array_sum_negative, %function
.section .text
array_sum_negative:
    // r0 contains the pointer to the array
    mov r1, #5              // Number of elements
    vsub.f64 d0, d0         // Initialize sum to 0.0
    vsub.f64 d2, d2         // Load 0.0 for comparison

loop:
    vldr.f64 d1, [r0]                // Load double from array
    vcmp.f64 d1, d2                  // Compare with 0.0
    vmrs APSR_nzcv, FPSCR   // Move floating-point flags to CPU flags
    it lt
    vaddlt.f64 d0, d0, d1            // Add to sum if negative
    add r0, r0, #8          // Increment pointer
    subs r1, r1, #1         // Decrement counter
    bne loop               // Continue if not zero
    bx lr                  // Return, sum is in d0
```

In this code, we use the sequence

```
it lt
vaddlt.f64 d0, d0, d1
```

in order to avoid branch.
Also, the label **skip_add** is removed.

Example 10

It is easily to modify the assembly function **array_sum_negative** to calculate the sum of positive elements of a 5-element array of double-precision floating-point numbers. The modified function named **array_sum_positive** is shown in **Listing 18**.

Listing 18.

```
.syntax unified
.arch armv8-a
.thumb
.global array_sum_positive
.type array_sum_positive, %function
.section .text
array_sum_positive:
    // r0 contains the pointer to the array
    mov r1, #5          // Number of elements
    vsub.f64 d0, d0     // Initialize sum to 0.0
    vsub.f64 d2, d2     // Load 0.0 for comparison
loop:
    vldr.f64 d1, [r0]            // Load double from array
    vcmp.f64 d1, d2             // Compare with 0.0
    vmrs APSR_nzcv, FPSCR   // Move floating-point flags to CPU flags
    it gt
    vaddgt.f64 d0, d0, d1    // Add to sum if positive
    add r0, r0, #8           // Increment pointer
    subs r1, r1, #1          // Decrement counter
    bne loop                // Continue if not zero
    bx lr                   // Return, sum is in d0
```

In this code, we change the sequence

```
it lt
vaddlt.f64 d0, d0, d1
```

from **array_sum_negative** to

```
it gt
vaddgt.f64 d0, d0, d1
```

The C caller for the function **array_sum_positive** looks like the following (**Listing 19**).

Listing 19.

```
#include <stdio.h>
#include <stdlib.h>
```

```
double a1[5] = { -2.12, 6.09, 1.03, -1.77, 7.46 };
double result;

extern double array_sum_positive(double *a1);

int main()
{
    result = array_sum_positive(a1);
    printf("Sum of positives = %f\n", result);
    return 0;
}
```

The application produces the following output:

Sum of positives = 14.580000

Example 11

In this example, the assembly function **find_first_negative (Listing 20)** searches for the first negative element in the 5-element double-precision floating-point array. If success, the procedure returns the index of this element, otherwise it returns -1.

Listing 20.

```
.syntax unified
.arch armv8-a
.thumb
.global find_first_negative
.type find_first_negative, %function
.section .text
find_first_negative:
    // r0 contains the pointer to the array
    mov r1, #5          // Number of elements
    mov r2, #0          // Initialize index counter
    vsub.f64 d2, d2     // Load 0.0 for comparison

loop:
    vldr.f64 d1, [r0]       // Load double from array
```

```
vcmp.f64 d1, d2        // Compare with 0.0
vmrs APSR_nzcv, FPSCR  // Move floating-point flags to CPU flags
bmi found_negative     // Branch if negative (N flag set)
add r0, r0, #8         // Increment pointer
add r2, r2, #1         // Increment index counter
subs r1, r1, #1        // Decrement element counter
bne loop               // Continue if not zero

// If we get here, no negative element was found
mov r0, #-1            // Return -1
bx lr

found_negative:
    mov r0, r2         // Move index to return value
    bx lr              // Return, index is in r0
```

Explanation

1. Use **r2** as an index counter, initialized to 0 by instruction `mov r2, #0`.
2. The instruction `vsub.f64 d2, d2` writes **0.0** into **d2** for comparison.
3. In the loop, we do the following:
   - Compare each element with 0.0.
   - Branch to **found_negative** if the number is negative (**N** flag is set).
   - Increment the index counter if not negative.
   - Continue the loop if we haven't found a negative number and haven't reached the end of the array.
4. If we exit the loop without finding a negative number, we set the return value (**r0**) to -1.
5. If we find a negative number, we jump to **found_negative**, where we move the current index (**r2**) to **r0** for returning.
6. The function returns the index in **r0** or -1.

This function will return the index (0 to 4) of the first negative element it finds in the 5-element array. If no negative element is found, it returns -1.

The C code that calls the function **find_first_negative** is shown in **Listing 21**.

Listing 21.

```c
#include <stdio.h>
#include <stdlib.h>

double a1[5] = { 9.22, 0.34, -4.67, -1.03, 88.21 };
int result;

extern int find_first_negative(double *a1);

int main()
{
    result = find_first_negative(a1);
    if (result == -1)
        printf("No negative element found.\n");
    else
        printf("Index of a first negative: %d\n", result);
    getchar();
    return 0;
}
```

The application produces the following output:

Index of a first negative: 2

Example 12

The assembly function **find_first_negative** can easily be modified to search for the first positive element in the 5-element double-precision floating-point array. If such element is found, the procedure returns the index of this element, otherwise it returns -1. The source code of the function named **find_first_positive** is shown in **Listing 22**.

Listing 22.

```asm
.syntax unified
.arch armv8-a
.thumb
.global find_first_positive
```

```
.type find_first_positive, %function
.section .text
find_first_positive:
    // r0 contains the pointer to the array
    mov r1, #5          // Number of elements
    mov r2, #0          // Initialize index counter
    vsub.f64 d2, d2     // Load 0.0 for comparison

loop:
    vldr.f64 d1, [r0]          // Load double from array
    vcmp.f64 d1, d2            // Compare with 0.0
    vmrs APSR_nzcv, FPSCR   // Move floating-point flags to CPU flags
    bpl found_positive     // Branch if positive
    add r0, r0, #8            // Increment pointer
    add r2, r2, #1            // Increment index counter
    subs r1, r1, #1          // Decrement element counter
    bne loop                 // Continue if not zero

    // If we get here, no positive element was found
    mov r0, #-1              // Return -1
    bx lr
found_positive:
    mov r0, r2              // Move index to return value
    bx lr                  // Return, index is in r0
```

In this code, we changed the instruction

bmi found_negative

from the function **find_first_negative** to

bpl found_positive

The C code that calls the function **find_first_positive** is shown in **Listing 23**.

Listing 23.

```
#include <stdio.h>
#include <stdlib.h>
```

```c
double a1[5] = { -9.22, -0.31, -4.67, 1.05, 88.21 };
int result;

extern int find_first_positive(double *a1);

int main()
{
    result = find_first_positive(a1);
    if (result == -1)
        printf("No positive element found.\n");
    else
        printf("Index of a first positive: %d\n", result);
    getchar();
    return 0;
}
```
The application produces the following output:

Index of a first positive: 3

Example 13

In this example, the assembly procedure **clear_negative (Listing 24)** searches for negative elements in a 5-element floating-point array and replaces each negative element with 0.0.

Listing 24.

```
.syntax unified
.arch armv8-a
.thumb
.global clear_negative
.type clear_negative, %function
.section .text
clear_negative:
    // r0 contains the pointer to the array
    mov r1, #5          // Number of elements
    mov r2, #0          // Initialize an index counter
    vsub.f64 d2, d2     // Load 0.0 for comparison
```

loop:

```
loop:
    vldr.f64 d1, [r0]         // Load double from the array
    vcmp.f64 d1, d2           // Compare with 0.0
    vmrs APSR_nzcv, FPSCR     // Move floating-point flags to CPU flags
    it mi
    vsubmi.f64 d1, d1         // If d1 < 0, replace it with 0.0
    vstr.f64 d1, [r0]         // Save d1 in memory
    add r0, r0, #8            // Increment the pointer
    add r2, r2, #1            // Increment the index counter
    subs r1, r1, #1           // Decrement the element counter
    bne loop                 // Continue if not zero
    bx lr                    // Return
```

The C code that calls the function **clear_negative** looks like the following (**Listing 25**).

Listing 25.

```
#include <stdio.h>
#include <stdlib.h>

double a1[5] = { 9.22, -0.34, 4.67, -1.03, 88.21};
extern void clear_negative(double *a1);

int main()
{
    clear_negative(a1);
    printf("Updated array:\n");
    for(int i = 0; i < 5; i++)
        printf("<%d>: %f\n", i, a1[i]);
    return 0;
}
```

The application produces the following output:

Updated array:
<0>: 9.220000
<1>: 0.000000
<2>: 4.670000
<3>: 0.000000

Example 14

In this example, we will modify the assembly function **clear_negative** to process positive elements of an 5-element floating-point array. The source code of the modified function named **clear_positive** is shown in **Listing 26**. This function searches for the positive elements in a 5-element array and replaces all such elements with 0.

Listing 26.

```
.syntax unified
.arch armv8-a
.thumb
.global clear_positive
.type clear_positive, %function
.section .text
clear_positive:
    // r0 contains the pointer to the array
    mov r1, #5        // Number of elements
    mov r2, #0        // Initialize an index counter
    vsub.f64 d2, d2   // Load 0.0 for comparison

loop:
    vldr.f64 d1, [r0]        // Load double from the array
    vcmp.f64 d1, d2          // Compare with 0.0
    vmrs APSR_nzcv, FPSCR   // Move floating-point flags to CPU flags
    it pl
    vldrpl.f64 d1, =0        // If d1 > 0, replace it with 0
    vstr.f64 d1, [r0]        // Save d1 in memory
    add r0, r0, #8          // Increment the pointer
    add r2, r2, #1          // Increment the index counter
    subs r1, r1, #1         // Decrement the element counter
    bne loop               // Continue if not zero
    bx lr                  // Return
```

The C code that calls the **clear_positive** function looks like the following (**Listing 27**).

225

Listing 27.

```c
#include <stdio.h>
#include <stdlib.h>

double a1[5] = { -9.22, 0.34, -4.67, -1.03, 88.21};
extern void clear_positive(double *a1);

int main()
{
    clear_positive(a1);
    printf("Updated array:\n");
    for(int i = 0; i < 5; i++)
        printf("<%d>: %f\n", i, a1[i]);
    return 0;
}
```

The application produces the following output:

Updated array:
<0>: -9.220000
<1>: 0.000000
<2>: -4.670000
<3>: -1.030000
<4>: 0.000000

INDEX

www.ingramcontent.com/pod-product-compliance
Lightning Source LLC
LaVergne TN
LVHW051323050326
832903LV00031B/3325